JUST BOURNEMOUTH

Just
BOURNEMOUTH

Keith Rawlings

THE DOVECOTE PRESS

Three Writers on Bournemouth

'An outlying eastern tract of enormous Egdon Waste . . . yet on the very verge of that tawny piece of antiquity such a glittering novelty as this pleasure city has chosen to spring up.'
Thomas Hardy

'When I am better tempered I shall like the old maids and the Philistine men and the very proper proprietous maidens right enough. It's always raining – so stupid of it.'
D.H. Lawrence

'I shall expire vulgarly at Bournemouth and they will bury me on the shore near the bandstand. I have been in this quiet place of invalids and gentlemanly sunsets for about 100 years, ever since yesterday week.'
Rupert Brooke

First published in 2005 by The Dovecote Press Ltd
Stanbridge, Wimborne Minster, Dorset BH21 4JD

ISBN 1 904349 39 0

© Keith Rawlings 2005

The author has asserted his rights under the Copyright, Designs and Patent Act 1988 to be identified as author of this work

Designed by The Dovecote Press
Printed and bound in Singapore

All papers used by The Dovecote Press are natural, recyclable products made from wood grown in sustainable, well-managed forests

A CIP catalogue record for this book is available from the British Library

1 3 5 7 9 8 6 4 2

Contents

Introduction

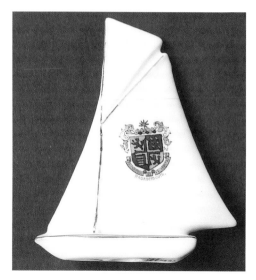

Once Bank Holidays were introduced in 1871, day trips to Bournemouth became popular. W.H. Goss at his pottery in Stoke-on-Trent produced miniature china ornaments as souvenirs. Two shops in Holdenhurst Road had pieces specially produced for them as they were on the route back to the railway station. Beales had designs produced with their name on the base and these are especially sought after. Above are a yacht, and one of three special designs of historic items dug up in Bournemouth, a 'pilgrim bottle' found at Southbourne.

Bournemouth has had its story told in a succession of books of photographs with a few lines of history under each photograph. This book attempts to tell the story of the town under obvious headings, with supplementary information placed in boxes alongside the main text. Sometimes quotations in italics have been made without acknowledgement; these were jotted in my notes over many years and my memory for their sources has now faded.

I have consulted most of the books I could find when writing this one. *Bournemouth: 1810-1910* by Mate and Riddle, published locally, and *The Story of Bournemouth* by David S. Young have both been invaluable. David and Rita Popham's *The Book of Bournemouth* has also been useful, and I commend these three to you. But they are difficult to come by and even secondhand copies are costing more than £50 at 2005 prices, and rising steadily. Of the picture books, Louise Perrin's *A Century of Bournemouth* and *Bournemouth Then and Now* by Peters, Couling and Ridley are the best. I regard the Further Reading at the end to be an essential part of this book.

The early guide books to Bournemouth are extremely rare. I have seen only one copy of *The Penny Guide to Bournemouth* which is a tiny 64 page booklet, including 22 pages of advertisements and 20 pages about Bournemouth, published by T.J. Powell, Commercial Road, and printed by Pardy & Co, Steam Printers, Bournemouth. Sydenham's *Illustrated and Descriptive Guide to Bournemouth and the Surrounding District*, the 15th Edition, published in 1884, includes a chapter called the 'Sanitary Character of Bournemouth', which reveals that Winton is 'mainly inhabited by mechanics and the labouring population of Bournemouth'. I live in Winton, and my neighbours may be shocked to read that.

A series of booklets published by the Bournemouth Local Studies Publications from the Teachers' Centre of about 30 years ago are fascinating to read. It is a shame that most titles are out of print and only some are available in the reference sections of Bournemouth libraries. It is possible to find the occasional copy lurking on a shelf of an independent bookseller, but they are usually repetitions of the same titles. I freely acknowledge the assistance these excellent publications have given me. No others have the detail provided in them about Bournemouth.

As for the stories and anecdotes, most of them have been heard over the years and jotted down on scraps of paper which fortunately I have preserved. Above all, I must thank Wally Driffield, MBE, for his readiness in supplying me with some of the longer stories which I have heard him use in the many talks on Bournemouth he has given.

My thanks are due to The Russell-Cotes Art Gallery and Museum and Shaun Garner, The Bournemouth Library and Jan Marsh, and The Planning Department of Bournemouth Council for permission to reproduce photographs and drawings and to Michael Stead. The section on Bournemouth Ghosts owes much to the late Dick Sheppherd who, when he was the publicity officer for Bournemouth, published through the Authority a duplicated booklet on the subject to supplement the talks he gave. John Bowen, former Chief Executive Officer for Bournemouth, and Adrian Fudge have been most helpful on more recent times. Scott Harrison of the *Daily Echo's* Library can give information about the town at the drop of a hat, and so too can David Harrison at the Town Hall. Hazel and Martin Thornby have gladly let me use pictures from their extensive collection of photographs of old Bournemouth which they exhibit in many parts of the town. John Barker very kindly read the typescript and made many helpful suggestions before publication. Tony and Deborah Orman willingly rushed in to transfer my typescript on to proper computer disks. Murray Rogers kindly photographed items from my Bournemouth collection. My wife, Eileen, was an assiduous corrector of proofs, took many of the photographs, and always encouraged me.

I must also thank those many men who, over a pint of beer, have readily regaled me with their memories of the past. That's true history.

Obviously, much on the modern era I have written about is from my own knowledge by being a member of Bournemouth Council for twenty years spread between 1970 and 2003. I hope I have been factual and not too politically biased.

Lastly, I'm a collector of books, badges and china relating to Bournemouth. Years ago I bought a job lot at a local auction sale and discovered a white metal armlet: 'Borough of Bournemouth Licensed Porter 22'. What was it used for? No one at the Town Hall could find any record of its issue. It was the same with a 22ct Gold Plated Medallion issued for the Bournemouth Borough Centenary as recently as 1990. I had one copy and wanted another to show the obverse side on a display board. The Town Hall did not know whether any more existed or even that they had been issued. But that's understandable. Staffs change: they retire or they move on to higher things elsewhere. Certainly no one had a copy preserved for posterity. That made me collect metal, plastic and cloth memorabilia, and some of the items I have assembled are reproduced in this book. It is my intention to mount them all and leave them to the Town, provided they can be displayed somewhere and not be buried away where no one can enjoy looking at them.

Please send me any stories you know which are not in this edition; and feel free to use any which are already printed. Enjoy the book.

KEITH RAWLINGS

Bournemouth, 2005

Conference Books

A leather-bound book called *Bournemouth* was issued as a souvenir of the Congress of the Royal Sanitary Institute in 1922. The British Medical Association published *The Book of Bournemouth* for their annual meeting in 1934. Both contain invaluable information about the town not found elsewhere. Nowadays, visiting conference delegates are greeted at a reception hosted by the mayor. Occasionally a 'Music Hall' is preferred, and the 'Hiss an' Boo' Company has been a popular choice in recent years.

Street Trading Licence, 42, County Borough of Bournemouth, probably issued during the 1920s.

Early Days

The Bourne Stream

Only the tributaries of the Bourne Stream from Branksome and Alderney are culverted. It is possible to see the main stream that runs from the Ringwood Road just to the east of the Mountbatten Arms through Bourne Bottom most of the way until it goes under the railway embankment and emerges into Coy Pond. They flow out of the Pond to form the Bourne Stream from which our town takes its name.

As Bournemouth is a young town it is easy to trace its history. It did not gradually expand from a Saxon or medieval village into a town. It grew at an ever accelerating pace on heathland in the early years of the nineteenth century, and was originally intended for the affluent and invalids.

The earliest reference to Bournemouth is in a Survey taken in 1574 by the Earl of Southampton of the coast of what was then the County of Southampton, from Hayling Island to Poole Harbour.

'First wee finde at Bornemouthe, within the west baye at Christchurch a place very easy for the ennemye to land there conteyning by estimacion oon quarter of a myle in length being voyde of all inhabiting.

Wee finde more a place called Bastowe [Boscombe] *within the sais Baye which is also an easy place for the ennemye to landed conteyning in length a Flight Shott.'*

Maps published only a few years later show Bourne Chine, Holenest, Parkstone, The Mynes, Allom Chine, Copperas House and Bascombe Copperas House and a Marine Store House at the mouth of the River Bourne – all of which seem to contradict the earl's assertion that the area was 'voyde of all inhabiting'.

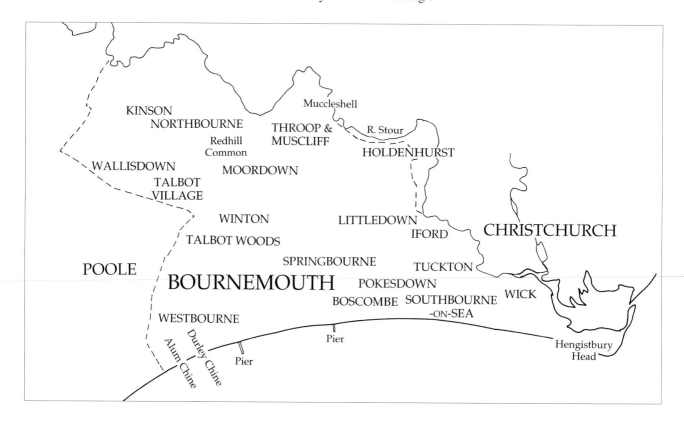

Smugglers at Bourne Mouth by H.P. Parker which used to hang in the Tregonwell Arms. The central figure is thought to be Isaac Gulliver.

But in truth, inhabitants were few, specially on the heath and near the sea. Small villages existed at Holdenhurst and Throop. Kinson was a hamlet, and elsewhere a handful of cottagers and smallholders eked out a precarious living on the heath. The principal landmark for travellers making the journey from Christchurch to Poole was a decoy house, known as Bourne House, which stood alongside a decoy pond for wildfowling.

The first attempt to profit from Bournemouth ended in disaster. In 1567 Lord Mountjoy of Canford Manor obtained the rights to extract alum and copperas from the aluminous shale beneath the heath. Despite promising to deliver Queen Elizabeth I 150 tons of alum and a share of anticipated annual profits of £4000 the venture was never a success. In 1577 the Queen's share amounted to £9. Four years later Lord Mountjoy died in poverty.

The other source of revenue from the area was smuggling. In Kinson churchyard is the tomb of Robert Trotman, 'barbarously murdered on the shore' by Revenue Officers in 1765; and the church tower and a false tomb were both used as smugglers' hiding places. The most celebrated local smuggling gang flourished in the second half of the eighteenth century under the leadership of Isaac Gulliver. Known as the 'White Wigs' because of their smock frocks and powdered wigs, Gulliver's gang landed their cargoes of tea and spirits on the beaches, before moving them inland via the chines and heath. After being pardoned in 1782, Gulliver settled down to enjoy the considerable fruits of his trade, dying respected and prosperous in 1822.

But despite Gulliver's retirement, smuggling continued. As late as 1821, nearly 200 casks of spirit which had been landed at Bourne Bottom were confiscated by the Revenue Officers, proof that the contraband trade flourished for a considerable time after the foundation of Bournemouth. The first lodging-house keepers were not averse to buying at a low price tea, spirits, and lace on which duty had never been paid.

For those living on the heath, smuggling was a means to an end. Much of the heath was unfenced common land. The soil was poor, providing

Industrial Scam
Bournemouth's first industry in the 17th century did not last long as it was based on a swindle. A man named Medley persuaded influential people, including the great Lord Burleigh, that he was able to make raw iron into copper, and that the liquor in which the iron was boiled would produce copperas and alum ready for use in tanning and in the manufacture of ink.

A more reputable production of alum existed on Brownsea Island and at Boscombe. The deposits found in the area of Alum Chine were usually marked with luxuriant holly bushes which seemed to thrive on alum.

only limited grazing. The commoners also had the right to cut turf for fuel, a right called turbary (hence Turbary Park Avenue and Turbary Road).

At certain times of the year their normal fare was replaced by fish, especially mackerel, great shoals of which were netted off Bourne Mouth. Cottagers and farmworkers left the fields for the beaches, and were paid in fish for helping to land and pack the catch. One evening in 1803, when they were hauling in the nets, a press-gang secured 60 labourers, who were taken to Poole to appear before a magistrate. Only those who had previously been to sea could be forced to join the Navy. Such were the magistrate's sympathies, that of the 60 only one was sent to sea.

The need for men for the Navy was largely the result of the outbreak of war with Napoleonic France. Ironically, it was also the catalyst for the events that set in motion Bournemouth's birth. Inevitably, the war had added to the importance of farming and the need to increase both the land in cultivation and its yields.

In 1801, the General Enclosure Act was passed by Parliament to make it easier for landlords who were prepared to farm the land to enclose and divide it up. Amongst the common land to be affected was the Liberty of Westover, which itself was a part of the Manor of Christchurch, and which then belonged to Sir George Ivison Tapps.

A year later, '*An Act for dividing, allotting, and inclosing certain commonable lands and waste grounds within the Parish of Christchurch and the Parish or Chapelry of Holdenhurst in the County of Southampton*' was presented to Parliament.

The Award was finally completed in 1805. After the administrative charges had been calculated, 1,258 acres were put up for sale by the Enclosure Commissioners. Forty-one commoners received allocations to compensate for their loss of common rights, some of whom bought additional acreage. There were seven principal purchasers of land, including the Earl of Malmesbury, Sir George Ivison Tapps, and William Dean (who bought 40% of the land sold at £1.25p an acre). Those who bought small amounts were a Christchurch doctor, a London speculator, the vicar of Canford Magna, and two genuinely local people: Philip Norris of Boscombe Cottage and Cornelius Trim who farmed at Throop.

The loss of their traditional rights, specially that of cutting turf for fuel, was hard on the cottagers dependent on the heath for their livelihood. William West of Muscliff Farm, a 'learned and considerate' farmer, helped them write a petition asking the Enclosure Commissioner to safeguard their rights to graze cattle and cut brushwood and turf. Five areas totalling 425 acres were placed in trust for their benefit: Seafield Gardens, Kings Park, Queens Park, Redhill Common and Meyrick Park. In 1889 they became the five parks of Bournemouth.

The 5,084 acres of heathland which had been divided up were too infertile to become agricultural land, and thus remained as heath until Captain Lewis Tregonwell bought land from Sir George Tapps for £21 an acre in 1810, then £40 in 1814. At a further sale in 1822 Sir George was delighted at being able to charge Tregonwell £60 an acre, on which he built marine cottages which he let to friends for the summer.

The Rustic Bridge across the stream which flowed along what is now Old Christchurch Road. The spot is marked today by the iron arch at St Peter's Walk at the north end of Bournemouth Arcade.

Captain Lewis Tregonwell

Lewis Dymock Grosvenor Tregonwell (1758-1832) is generally thought of as the 'founder' of Bournemouth. As an officer in the Dorset Yeomanry, Tregonwell had first 'discovered' Bourne Mouth when in command of a troop of Yeomanry responsible for defending the area against possible invasion by Napoleon.

He returned to it again in the summer of 1810 with his second wife, Henrietta, on a trip from Mudeford, where they had been staying, to show her an area he had come to know well when an active soldier. They probably stayed in the Tapps Arms, opened the previous year and the first building to be built in Bournemouth since the granting of the Enclosure Award in 1805. Tregonwell was later to rebuild the inn, renaming it the Tregonwell Arms.

Henrietta Tregonwell fell in love with the still desolate coastal landscape, even then almost entirely encircled with pine trees. Inland, heath and heather attracted bees and '*yielded so bountiful a harvest of honey for the benefit of cottagers for miles around'*.

Encouraged by his wife, the Captain – whose main home was in Cranborne – immediately bought 8½ acres from Sir George Tapps. On it he built Bournemouth's first private house, originally known as the 'mansion', which still survives as part of the Royal Exeter Hotel.

Captain Lewis Tregonwell, the founder of Bournemouth.

Below Left Tregonwell's house in about 1811. Parts of it are now incorporated into the Royal Exeter Hotel, opposite the Bournemouth International Centre.

Tregonwell died aged 73 in January 1832. On his tomb in St. Peter's churchyard it celebrates his being *'the first to bring Bournemouth into notice as a watering place by erecting a mansion for his own occupation, having been his favourite retreat for many years before his death'*.

He also built a cottage for his butler called Portman Lodge, which remained on a site opposite The Moon in the Square until 1922 when it burned down. The Hants and Dorset Bus Station which replaced it also burned down. It was in this cottage that his widow, who was a daughter of Henry Portman, grandfather of the 1st Viscount Portman, died in 1846.

Tregonwell was an astute business man. As well as his own house, he built some four or five cottages *'which he lets to persons who go sea-bathing'*. He lived in the 'mansion' for only a few years, eventually letting it to the Marchioness of Exeter (hence its later name of Exeter House). He and his wife moved into the cottage they had built for their gardener, later enlarging it, on the site now occupied by the Melville Hotel.

Above right Portman Lodge in 1863.

Above The statue of Lewis Tregonwell given to the town by the Mayor and Mayoress of Bournemouth (Keith and Eileen Rawlings) 1998-1999. Tregonwell holds a bucket and spade as the founder of the popular seaside resort, and a scroll bearing the names of the three locally born holders of the Victoria Cross. On the other side of it is C.C. Creeke (Jonathan Sells, sculptor).

Samuel Bayly

By 1836 other speculators had moved in, including David Tuck and Samuel Bayly (1798-1864), the latter becoming the owner of the Belle Vue boarding house on the site where the present Pavilion now stands. Bayly was a Christchurch draper who had made enough money to retire early to Hengistbury House, the house he built at Purewell.

As well as a villa, Bayly also acquired *'a strip of land, near the beach on the west side of the River Bourne at Bournemouth, measuring about 300 feet in length, with the exclusive right of Bathing, and of Standing Machines for Bathing on the Beach, for half a mile on each side of the River, together with three buildings under the cliff in front of the Bourne Baths and four Bathing Machines'*.

Bayly would have been wiser to enjoy his retirement. The business was not a success, and a few years later he was forced to sell all his properties at auction to clear his debts. He later opened a wine merchants in Commercial Road, but never regained his lost capital.

Tapps Arms/Tregonwell Arms Inn.

The Tapps Arms was built by Sir George Tapps in 1809. Situated at what is now the junction of Post Office Road and St. Peter's Way, it was the only place of refreshment between Iford and Poole, and a popular meeting place for local smugglers.

Later, Sir George sold some of the land and the Inn to Lewis Tregonwell, who rebuilt and renamed it. When Tregonwell died in 1832, his widow leased the inn to George Fox, and five years later he bought it from her. In 1839 Fox became the Receiver of Letters and a post office was established at the Inn. The letters were sorted on the bar counter for the appropriately named Mr. Satchell, the postman who came in each day from Poole to collect the mail.

In 1866 the Poole Methodist Circuit built a chapel next to the Inn, and when in 1884 the then licensee retired, the Methodists purchased the Inn with the intention of demolishing it to build a larger chapel. Prior to demolition, it became the Blue Ribbon Gospel Temperance Coffee House. However, the Methodists did not build on the site; their new chapel was erected on Richmond Hill, and called the Punshon Memorial Church. This was destroyed by enemy action in 1943 and was later rebuilt in Exeter Road.

Sir George William Tapps-Gervis

Following the death of his father in 1835, his son George succeeded as Lord of the Manor of Westover and inherited the family's estates, also adding Gervis to his name.

Sir George soon began developing his Bourne Mouth estate. The Christchurch-born architect, Benjamin Ferrey, was commissioned to draw up plans which included roads, the Belle Vue boarding house, the Bath Hotel and Westover Villas, a dozen of which were built on the east side of the Bourne Stream on land sloping down to the sea. Much more might have been achieved but for Sir George's early death in 1842. Management of the estate devolved to trustees who appointed Decimus Burton, the designer of the Arch at Hyde Park Corner, as architect. It was Burton who suggested that much of the central land either side of the Bourne Stream should be laid out as pleasure gardens, which have ultimately proved to be one of the town's most successful and enduring features. Gates and rustic bridges were constructed and in due course a charge was made for entry to the Gardens.

An early design by Benjamin Ferry for the Gervis Estate in the 1840s. Much of it was never realised. Tregonwell's 'mansion' is the large house on the left.

One of Bournemouth's rustic bridges which crossed the River Bourne in about 1865. In the background on the right is 'Brookside', the house in which the poet and theologian John Keble died. Today it is the Hermitage Hotel, Exeter Road.

Dr. A.B. Granville

Dr. Granville was the author of the popular *The Spas of England*, first published in 1841 with no mention of Bournemouth. Sir George Tapps-Gervis invited the doctor to stay with him in the hope that in future editions the town would be mentioned. The invitation paid off. In the second edition, the doctor wrote: *'I look upon Bournemouth and its yet unformed colony as a perfect discovery among the sea nooks one longs to have. No situation that I have had occasion to examine on the whole southern coast possesses as many capabilities'*. Sir George's estate rose in value, as readers flocked to Bournemouth in hopes of buying land and building a house.

Memories

My grandfather lived in Bournemouth and so did my father, and I was born here over 80 years ago. So I remember stories of the development of this very young town.
The Meyricks and the Deans had the land, but what was on top of it was developed and bought in small lots by working class men: carpenters, bricklayers journeymen – rough and ready men who saw a chance to get rich quickly. And why shouldn't they? The owners of the land got their cut.
  A.H. (Retired Estate Agent & Surveyor)

This mixture of informality and rustic charm shaped Bournemouth's early growth. In his plans, Decimus Burton wrote, *'I am aware that houses of a large scale are particularly enquired for . . . and in designing a building plan for Bournemouth, formality should be carefully avoided'*.

He was particularly astute when he added, *'The characteristic which distinguishes Bournemouth from other watering places is its rusticity'*.

Curiously, Mrs. Richard Grosvenor in her play of 1815, *A Peep into the Futurity, or Small talk at Bourne some 60 years hence*, set in an imaginary Bournemouth of 1876, referred to 'the new bridge over the River Bourne, raised by the voluntary subscriptions of the fashionable residents of this frequented and distinguished bathing place'. A tiny bridge called the Bourne Plank over the Bourne Stream in the Square existed in the mid-18th century. Pedestrians walked across it; carriages and horse riders had to splash through the water. This bridge was known as Holdenhurst Bridge as late as 1856.

Mrs Grosvenor was remarkably far-sighted, for when she wrote her play there was scant evidence of a 'distinguished bathing place'. Yet by the time of Decimus Burton much had changed. Bournemouth was not yet fashionable, but one visitor was able to state that it would only be the townspeoples' fault if it didn't soon become 'an object of general admiration and attraction.'

Many books on the early days of Bournemouth paint a picture of wealthy people in large houses or villas, looked after by an army of butlers, cooks, maids, and gardeners – all of whom lived in. Before the arrival of the railway, food was provided by local farmers who produced milk and eggs and slaughtered their own cattle. Cottagers grew extra vegetables and reared the occasional chicken. But who built the houses? And more importantly where did these people live? A daily walk there and back to Poole, to Christchurch or to Ringwood on dirt tracks was unrealistic. As Bournemouth grew, so did the semi-circle of satellite communities that surround the town away from the sea. The first artisan houses were built in the Orchard Street (the only 'street' in the town) area and then in Springbourne and Winton.

The demand for bricklayers, carpenters, plasterers and plumbers must have been insatiable; the din of construction undoubtedly disturbing the tranquillity that was one of the town's principal attractions. It was not

The Belle Vue Hotel, Baths and the Pier Approach, about 1865.

class distinction alone that pushed the working class away from the large houses and villas. The growth of Bournemouth was phenomenal, with the sea taking the place of steelworks and health-giving pines the place of coal mines and factories.

As the town grew, its inhabitants became increasingly impatient to control their own destiny. On paper, it was still a part of the parish of Holdenhurst. But its needs were much more complex than those of a rural backwater. A meeting at the Belle Vue Hotel was followed by an application to Parliament for an Act 'for the improvement of Bournemouth'. It became law in July 1856, granting the town a measure of self-government and placing responsibility for its administration in the hands of 13 Commissioners, of which one was to be the Lord of the Manor.

'It is expedient that provision should be made for the more efficient paving, sewerage, drainage, lighting, cleansing, watching, and otherwise improving part of the district of St. Peter's, Bournemouth, in the Parishes of Christchurch and Holdenhurst, in the County of Southampton, and for holding markets therein, and for providing a pier.'

The second section of the Act limited the jurisdiction of the Commissioners to 'a circle of the radius of ONE MILE, whereof the centre is the front door of the Belle Vue Hotel'. This Hotel was where the Pavilion now stands.

Lord Abercrombie later commented this was a ridiculous place to be the centre as it excluded much of the area which needed to be developed, but it took until 1931 before the Borough as we know it today came under the jurisdiction of the Local Council.

Christopher Crabbe Creeke

The Bournemouth Improvement Act of 1856 thrust one of the most unlikely of men centre stage. Christopher Crabbe Creeke (1820-1886) had arrived in Bournemouth four years earlier aged 32, replacing Decimus Burton as Surveyor. Unlike the other principal figures in the town's early history, he didn't own any land – but it was Crabbe's influence that largely dictated what went on top of it. As well as Surveyor, Architect and Civil Engineer to the Commissioners, he was also Inspector of Nuisances, all

Above The statue of C.C. Creeke, behind that of Tregonwell. Creeke sits on a lavatory as Bournemouth's first Inspector of Nuisances. The sculptor was Jonathan Sells of Corfe. The statue is much used as a photographic background by students of Bournemouth University in their newly awarded cap and gown after their graduation ceremony held in the BIC.

Above right Lainston Villa in 1863. This was the home of C.C. Creeke and was also used by the Commissioners for their meetings. It stood at the corner of Exeter Road and Exeter Lane. It became the Garden Tea House until the 1920s, when it was demolished to become the Bus Station which was later destroyed by fire. It is now part of a car park opposite The Moon in The Square.

for a salary of £50 a year. It was he who prepared the plans that shaped Bournemouth's character in the second half of the nineteenth century, providing endless drawings and specifications to reinforce his vision of what the town could become.

He started with the roads, and it is their pattern that we notice today. They wind. There is hardly a straight road in any part of Bournemouth for which Crabbe masterminded the plans. He had a particular fondness for serpentine bends and crescents. Even today those taking short cuts by car can easily become lost. Because most of the area was hilly, gangs of navvies were set to work levelling, dumping the soil over the cliffs.

In addition to his civic duties, Crabbe managed Clapcott Dean's estate and the Branksome estate. He was also a busy private architect and was responsible for the present Lansdowne Baptist Church, the Wimborne Road Cemetery Chapel, the house which became the cramped Registry Office at Lorne Park Road (until it thankfully shifted into the Town Hall in 2004), and the Talbot Village Almshouses. He also found time to be a Captain in the Local Rifle Volunteers for nearly twenty years. His name is recorded on one of the tablets in the former Holdenhurst Road Drill Hall.

When he finally retired in 1879, he successfully stood for election as a Commissioner. Russell-Cotes believed that it was Creeke who had drawn the map of Bournemouth. He presented the town with a marble bust of Creeke to be placed in the Town Hall, but it languished in the vaults of his Museum until it was displayed for a year in the Mayor's Parlour in 1998, more than a century after his death.

The Pines

Bournemouth's acid soils are excellent for the pine and by 1840 many thousands had been planted, particularly on land belonging to Sir George Tapps-Gervis. Initially most were Scots pine, but it was soon found that the Maritime pine was less prone to suffering from lack of water and, by and large, it is the Maritime pine that today gives so much of old

The Constitutional Club, 38 Richmond Hill (1838). The only villa in the town to survive in its original form.

Bournemouth its character. An early guide described the area as 'The Forest City', another as 'Pine City'. Some local historians estimate that altogether 3 million pines were planted during the Victorian period, and their scent was very much regarded as one of Bournemouth's virtues. Breathing in the aroma of pines was thought of as healthy, adding to its popularity as a 'winter residence for the most delicate constitutions requiring a warm and sheltered locality'.

The tree's reward was to be put on the top of the town's badge, whilst its motto, *Pulchritudo et Salubritas* (Beauty and Health) re-inforced those early attractions.

A London doctor, Horace Dobell, who later moved his practice to Bournemouth, advised patients with pulmonary complaints to spend their winters in the town. After all, he argued, the Romans sent patients with ulcerated lungs to Libya, where, *'by breathing the balsamic effluvia of the pines, with which the country abounded, they are said to have lived many years in safety from their complaints'*.

In 1885 Dr. Dobell estimated the number of pine trees still left in the different districts of Bournemouth to be as follows:

'Branksome Park Estate: 3,388,000 planted, 1,150,000 now standing.

Talbot Woods: plantation on the north side 150,000 still standing (eighty years old).

Durrant Estate: The whole of it was once clothed, but about twenty-eight years ago nearly all the trees were destroyed by fire . . . The number will be about 9,000 for the district westward of the bridge in the Square.

East Cliff and Boscombe Estates: (estimated by Messrs. Rebbeck), about 400,000.

Southbourne-on-Sea and the adjoining estates of Stourcliff, Stornwood, Carbery, Stourfield, Mr. Hunter's Estate, etc., about 250,000. Mr. Clapcott Dean's, Messrs. Kemp Welch's, and a few other Estates – estimates not rendered.'

The Winter Garden of England

'Twenty five years ago it would perhaps have been difficult to credit that the little village of Bournemouth – with its barren, uncultivated heath and its dense pine woods – would in a few years spring up into one of the most fashionable and picturesque watering-places in England. And yet, when one becomes acquainted with the picturesque surroundings of

Invalids' Walk, now Pine Walk, 1875. This type of walk was a popular feature of the town for many years.

Flaming June

A deputation was sent to rival resorts in England and on the continent to report to the Council on the buildings provided for visitors. The Kursaal at Ostend was built at enormous expense by its municipality for a season that lasted just over two months from July to the middle of September.

'Our season in Bournemouth', said the Town Clerk at a public meeting, 'lasts for eleven months in the year'.

The Inspector: 'Which is the month that drops out?'

Town Clerk: 'It is June. They do not come here as they imagined it was hot. But after living here in the place for a number of years I can say there is no more delightful place in June than Bournemouth'. (December, 1909)

Bournemouth, its balmy air, its sunny days, its pleasant gardens, its pier, its bracing sea breezes, its pleasant situation in the middle of a crescent-shaped bay, with a full south aspect, its delightfully sandy beach (most safe for bathing), its rugged cliffs – bounded on the left by Christchurch Head, with the Isle of Wight and its far-famed Needles in the distance, and on the right by Poole Harbour, the Studland Heights, and the Old Harry Rocks – it may be conscientiously said that the only wonder is that such a lovely spot has not been planned and built upon years ago.

The medical testimony in reference to this climate as a health resort is extensive . . . medical authorities are unanimous in saying that this is the first watering-place in England, and, what is more, not only a watering-place, but a most suitable residence for delicate constitutions requiring a warm and sheltered locality. The East Cliff is perhaps the most sheltered, whilst the West Cliff is the more bracing . . . .

A peculiarity exists in regard to the temperature of the latter cliff viz, that while on the whole it is warmer in the winter, it is notably cooler in the summer than the East Cliff or other parts of the town; so that all persons may find whatever variety of temperature their constitutions demand. The restorative powers of the air – more particularly for chest complaints – is well known, and, ascribed to the favoured share of sunshine and its freedom from humidity, there are hardly a dozen days in the year but what the most delicate invalid can take outdoor exercise.'

from *Galignani's Messenger*, Paris, 1877

TWO

Victorian Heyday

Finally a Borough

By 1880 Bournemouth's population had grown to nearly 17,000. The arrival of the railway had accelerated its transformation from marine village to bustling town. No longer could its seafront be described as a place 'where a few damsels from time to time tripped down to bathe, secure from the ogling glances of impertinent observers.' Central Bournemouth was still largely residential, but commerce and business were beginning to have an impact on the town's appearance. The modern shops of Southbourne Terrace on the east side of the Square provided everything from freshly baked pastries to a new watch, from glass and china to 'ornamental hair' and French perfume. Lansdowne Crescent had been built, and a parade of shops opened for the new houses being built along the upper part of Old Christchurch Road, as well as Holdenhurst and Lansdowne Roads.

Population of Bournemouth

1841 - 405	1851- 695
1861 - 1,701	1871 - 5,896
1881 - 16,859	1891 - 59,762
1911 - 78,674	1921 - 91,761
1931 - 116,803	1939 - 144,451
1951 - 154,956	1961 - 155,620
1971 - 153,425	1981 - 144,803
1991 - 151,302	2001 - 163,444

Note the fall over the 30 years between 1961 and 1991, followed by the sudden rise.

Two views of Southbourne Terrace. The one on the left was taken in 1865, the one below from Terrace Mount in 1870 prior to the laying out of the Gardens. It shows the Scotch (Presbyterian) Church in the foreground and, to its right, the row of shops which now contains W.H. Smith. The church at the top of the picture is St Peter's Church before the spire was added.

Perpetual Committees
By 1903 there were 15 main committees, and, within another decade, a total of 19 sub-Committees with some strange but functional names, including Street Watering; Trees in Roads; Rifle Range; Flare Plates (sic); Cabmen's Shelters; Lunatic Asylum Committee; and a Horse, Hackney Carriage and Diseases of Animals Acts Committee.

In a Nutshell
'Unlike many market towns with an historic centre, which lends itself to conservation, the development of Bournemouth is essentially the joining up of a number of small settlements with infilling blurring the original boundaries. The oldest settlements are Kinson and Holdenhurst. Others, like Moordown, Iford and Pokesdown, grew around farms; and Winton, Boscombe and Springbourne were essentially dormitories to service Bournemouth. The establishment of Conservation Areas has helped to define those neighbourhoods which have a distinctive architectural and a definable style and form worth preserving or conserving.'
John Barker, Chairman, Bournemouth Civic Society.

The Growth of Bournemouth
Bournemouth proper in 1856 comprised 1,140 acres.
In 1876 Springbourne and much of Boscombe were joined to it.
In 1884, the rest of Boscombe, Westbourne and part of Malmesbury Park were added.
Pokesdown, Southbourne, Winton and Moordown were added in 1901.
Queen's Park, Lower Charminster and Strouden became part of the town in 1914.
Holdenhurst and Kinson followed in 1931, and Hengistbury Head in 1932.
Bournemouth now covers 11,627 acres.

Keeping Bournemouth Select
When, in 1856, a Board of Commissioners was appointed to implement the terms of the Bournemouth Improvement Act, it seems that the members were keen to keep the area select. Their influence was limited to within a mile radius of the Belle Vue Boarding House, but they always referred to it as an Hotel. When a cemetery was needed, land was acquired just outside the area. When a gas works was built, this, too, was outside the Commissioners' area. They would not countenance working-class houses: these were built at Springbourne, Winton and Boscombe, which, in those days, were not parts of Bournemouth.

The same criterion was applied when the railway reached Bournemouth. The station was built just outside the Commissioners' area in Holdenhurst Road.

Beyond the boundaries of the area directly administered by the Commissioners piecemeal development was beginning to disturb the once wild heathland and coastal chines (*see* chapter 14). Some enjoyed a brief period of independence, before Bournemouth's greater administrative influence gradually brought them within its orbit – usually by boundary extension (as with Boscombe and Springbourne in 1876).

It was against this background that an Act of 1882 allowing towns the right to petition for a charter conferring borough status was seized on by some local worthies as a panacea for Bournemouth's future. The town's expansion was outpacing its local government. If the town was to prosper it needed to widen its powers of self-government. A committee was formed 'to collect evidence and report on the advisability of applying for a Municipal Charter of Incorporation'. But at the Public Meeting held in the Town Hall (the Criterion Arcade), an enthusiastic majority was opposed by the Commissioners themselves ('our existence will be threatened'), and by a trio of its most powerful citizens and landowners: Sir George Meyrick, Sir Percy Shelley and Earl Cairns.

The advocates of reform were not easily defeated. Lead by a prominent developer, Joseph Cutler, and a former vicarage gardener, Enoch White, they forced the Commissioners to increase their number and divide the district into wards. But the battle for incorporation was not won so easily. Although a petition in favour (1,100 for, 934 against) was put forward, the Privy Council refused the application. Two further petitions were rejected, but by 1888 the number opposing the application had fallen to twenty and Hampshire County Council, of which Bournemouth was then a part, had withdrawn its initial objection.

The Charter was sealed on 23 July 1890. Five weeks later, eleven of the Commissioners travelled to the Home Office in London to receive it. To celebrate, the local clergy had been asked to supply the Commissioners with a list of old people 'for whom the gift of half a crown would be acceptable' (120 were distributed). Every child in the town was presented with a medal specially struck for the occasion (3,449 issued), whilst police officers were given two shillings (10p) and employees of the Commissioners one shilling.

There was also a pageant whose principal theme was the centuries prior

The first jetty known as the Pier in 1855. The Belle Vue Hotel is shown, but the perspective is distinctly inaccurate.

The First Jetty
This is a tramway on piles so that the top or platform is six feet wide and 100 feet long. The causeway to it is ten feet wide, and contains a similar rail to receive the jetty platform. When run off its bearing on the pile the platform is protected by a cord run through iron standards.
Guide to Bournemouth, Phillip Brannon, 1855.

to Bournemouth's foundation. 'A large number of horses and trollies' were requested from tradesmen and 150 'reliable men' put themselves forward to act the roles of England's monarchs – of whom the most important was King Alfred, in recognition of Winchester having England's oldest Charter.

The pageant started on the common at the rear of Bournemouth East Railway Station. Horsedrawn fire engines lead the procession, followed by eight bands. Carpenters and joiners carried a coffin, whilst at the rear local civic dignitaries rode in a carriage. The Charter was committed to the care of the Town Clerk and read by him to all those present. Civic pride satisfied, everyone repaired to the Mont Dore Hotel and a celebratory banquet.

Election Results, 1890
'The provisional Mayor read the results outside the Havergal Hall where the counting had taken place, standing on a chair, using matches to see the results. As the vestas sometimes went out in the middle of the reading, the crowd were kept on the tenterhooks of expectation.'
Havergal Hall was part of the then YWCA in Post Office Road, and much used for meetings and entertainments of the more serious kind as the building was controlled by the Strict Baptists.

The Piers

No self-respecting coastal resort without a harbour could possibly thrive without a pier. 'Go to sea and not feel seasick' ran their early publicity, satisfying the belief in the medicinal qualities of sea air with none of the attendant hazards of actually putting to sea.

Bournemouth's first pier was no more than a wooden landing jetty built on piles and paid for by public subscription. It had a retractable platform on the sand which allowed it to open or close for business. It certainly existed in 1855 but within five years it had been replaced by a proper pier. This had no building on it, just a few small shelters on each side in which to rest or shelter from the rain.

Despite being started before the contract had been signed, the new pier had a chequered history. Its designer, John Rennie (later knighted for his rebuilding of Waterloo Bridge) and the contractor disagreed; storms destroyed much of what had been built; and the bank, in which the town's funds had been placed, failed. This was especially embarrassing as the

Pigeon Post
In the early 1900s an ice cream manufacturer, Mr. H. Sparrack Smith, operated a stall on Bournemouth beach which was run by his son. Each day he took a basket of pigeons with him and, when stocks began to run low, Smith Jnr. would release one of the pigeons, which flew home to Palmerston Road in Boscombe, where the ice cream was made, and a fresh supply was sent to replenish the stall.

In 1875 a hut for refreshments was already being built near Bournemouth Pier.

bank was Legard & Sons (Poole Town and County Bank) and George Legard was Chairman of the Bournemouth Commissioners. Once complete its piles were attacked by the toredo shipworm. Even iron replacements did not save it from successive storm damage, which in 1867 swept away its T-head and 300 feet, and in 1876 destroyed a further 100 feet and made it impossible for steamers to moor alongside. Most of the 100 feet of timber was swept ashore at Swanage. It was acquired by Joseph Cutler, who used it to build Joseph's Steps, a flight of steps from the shore to the cliff top, better known today as the West Cliff Zig Zag.

Despite arguments as to the need for a pier at all, a new iron-built Bournemouth Pier was started in 1878 to the designs of C.E. Birch, and opened in 1880 by the then Lord Mayor of London. It was 858 feet long and 35 feet wide, *'terminating with a very capacious hexagonal head, surrounded by inclined and most convenient landing-stages, for the embarkation and disembarkation of passengers from steam vessels and pleasure boats'*. (Sydenham, 1886.) There was a small bandstand at the end with canvas awnings drawn by ropes over half the width to shelter the crowds from the sun or a sudden downpour. By the late 1890s roller skating had become a national craze, so special flooring was laid on part of the pier for skating on Tuesday and Friday afternoons.

Tolls were 1d, and in each of the years 1892/3, just over £6,000 was taken, nearly one and a half million paid admissions! (240d to the £1 in those days.) In 1912, a contributor to the *Hampshire Magazine* wrote: *'For a pier toll I could spend all day on Bournemouth Pier and see three variety shows and hear two municipal orchestras all for those coppers'*.

By 1929, toll charges had risen to 2d and a book of 12 tickets cost ls/8d. Enterprising children would buy a bookfull and sell the tickets

The Bournemouth Pier in 1872 after the destruction of its end by a gale. Gas lighting was installed a year later. The *Heather Belle* is leaving for its trip to Swanage.

The Pier and Belle Vue Hotel. At its left is the 'Public Baths' and on the right a 'Saloon Lounge'. This photograph dates from about 1920.

individually to make a handsome profit.

Pier Masters were important people, and the post carried considerable status. In the 1930s, the First Officer on the *Aquitania*, Captain A.J. Moss, was appointed to the position.

Excursion steamer trips were hugely popular – indeed the principal purpose of Bournemouth's piers was as a landing stage. The first regular steamer service was provided by the *Heather Belle,* whose passengers on its first voyage from Bournemouth in 1871 were serenaded by two bands. By 1880 two companies were competing for the Bournemouth trade during the season, Cosens of Weymouth and the Bournemouth South Coast Steam Packet Company. Paddle steamers came and went, but some had quite remarkable histories. The *Bournemouth* was wrecked after running aground in fog on Portland. The *Empress* completed the round trip to Torquay in a single day, taking 13½ hours. The *Stirling Castle* was sunk in the Mediterranean in 1916 and its sister ship, the *Windsor Castle,* had three name changes, one of them Russian, before ending its days off Japan. The *Waverley*, the world's last sea-going paddle steamer and now operated by a preservation society, served in both World Wars and still sails from Bournemouth on special occasions.

Bolson's Jetty, about 30 yards east of the pier, was built on large wheels, and used for smaller *Skylark* and *Titlark* trips round the Bay. Nearby, a raft was moored about 100 yards from the beach so that swimmers could climb up its steps, rest and use it for diving. Health and Safety regulations eventually demanded its removal.

Public Notice

The notice on this ramshackle building at the Pier Approach reads: *County Borough of Bournemouth. These buildings erected in 1876 will be demolished at the end of the 1936 season and a magnificent new sea and sun bathing establishment will be erected on the site by the Corporation.*

The *Windsor Castle* paddle steamer, 244 feet long and built in 1891, used Bournemouth Pier as its starting point for many trips along the coast.

Respectable By-Laws, 1900

Bathing machines must be capable of being moved by horse, windlass or by other animal or mechanical power so that the machine may be moved into such a depth of water as will prevent any indecent exposure of any person when bathing from the machine.

Where men only are permitted to bathe they must wear suitable drawers or other sufficient dress or covering to prevent indecent exposure of the person.

Where mixed bathing is permitted men should wear a suitable costume or dress (from the neck to the knees). Women must use a tent for changing in at all times.

The rebuilding of part of Bournemouth Pier after its deliberate demolition during the Second World War to hinder a threatened invasion.

Boscombe Pier

The drawbacks to the success of this undertaking (The Pier) have arisen from its somewhat unattractive character and the existence of a steep hill from the sea to the adjoining main thoroughfares. The Council is alive to these defects and is striving to counteract them as far as possible . . . Motor omnibuses are provided to convey visitors who desire to avoid the hill.

From an 1881 Review in *The Argosy*

The Pier seems wide, new, and well-built – place where one may pace up and down and enjoy the beauties of sunrise or sunset with the restless sea moving and surging around. Often one may have it to oneself as the visitors are most of them too delicate to venture thereon, except when the mid-day sun has dispersed all chilliness from the atmosphere.

Like most piers along the south coast, engineers blew away part of the pier's middle superstructure during the Second World War to prevent it being used by the enemy. When Boscombe Pier was restored, a building was placed at the end which was used latterly for roller skating until the whole structure was declared unsafe and suitable only for beach department storage. It has been unused by the public for nearly 30 years. In 2006, work on the restoration of the pier with surrounding leisure facilities and the construction of a surf reef are scheduled to begin. The 1600 feet long surf reef will be created from hundreds of sunken, specially constructed sandbags, consistently producing 6 feet high waves throughout the winter. In summer, bathers will enjoy the lagoon effect created by the reef. All this will be paid for by the sale of Honeycombe Chine for development into flats. Plans had to be redesigned because in 2005 the shops at the pier entrance were declared to be a listed building, much to everyone's surprise.

The Pier Theatre on Bournemouth Pier was opened in 1957, attracting well-known stars, mostly in farces and light entertainment shows during the season; by the 1990s the theatre rarely made a profit. The Show Bar and Amusement Arcade opened in 1981, ever since when they have produced yearly profits in excess of half a million pounds for the Council tax payers' benefit. Various schemes have been put forward at the request of the Council for private companies to develop the whole pier but, until 2004, all those submitted have been rejected, so for the moment at least it continues as normal.

The Promenade (Undercliff Drive)

Bournemouth's founding fathers promoted the construction of a promenade from soon after the town was established, if only to help protect the cliffs from erosion. There were also complaints from invalids, whose donkey-drawn carts often became stuck in the sand, and *'the loud and continuous drumming of boys with their sticks on the donkeys' ribs ought to be melancholy music to the patient who occupies the little four-wheeled chair'* (Grantley Berkeley, 1865).

Despite the support of Christopher Creeke, the merits of a promenade found little favour with many local residents, whose objections delayed its construction for the best part of fifty years. A private company's attempt to provide 'an esplanade, aquarium, boating club house and museum' between the pier and Durley Chine foundered. The Commissioners eventually put the design out for public competition and 29 designs were received, none of which met with unanimous approval. Nor were the ground landlords, Sir George Meyrick and Clapcott Dean, keen either. Sir George's interests stretched from the East Cliff as far as the Highcliffe Hotel, whilst Clapcott Dean owned from the hotel to Alum Chine. Without their support nothing was possible. Anyway, should any new drive be just a road, or ought there to be 'facilities' along it?

Eventually a Ratepayers' Undercliff Drive Promotion Association was formed with such local worthies as the Mayor and Merton Russell-Cotes serving on it. They published a pamphlet setting out the points in the promenade's favour, and a former Chairman of the Commissioners, Captain James Hartley, used the local press to remind the town that an Undercliff Drive *'was about all that was necessary to place Bournemouth in the very front rank of English health resorts, and enable us to compete with the attractions of the Riviera and other places abroad.'*

Then came a heavy cliff fall in 1896. The Council passed a motion to ask Sir George Meyrick to pass his interest in the cliffs and foreshore to the Council so they could proceed with the construction of the Undercliff. This he finally agreed to do in 1903, vesting his rights to the Council for 999 years, starting from 1902, as long as work was started within ten years. But it was not until 1907 that the first section of the Promenade was

For the many invalids who flocked to Bournemouth in search of health, bathchairs were available. These were wheeled carriages powered by a man, a boy, a donkey, a pony, even occasionally goats. A favoured route was from the Square, along Invalids' Walk to the beach or to the Bath Hotel for morning coffee or afternoon tea.

In 1914 there were no fewer than 101 bathchair proprietors, many of whom owned more than one vehicle. By the 1940s only six were licensed, classified as Hackney Carriages.

Bathing Machines
Bathing machines were like huts on wheels with a door at each end. A horse would pull the 'machine' to the water's edge and the bather would enter, close the door, undress, then leave by means of the door on the seaward side. In the early days of sea bathing, nudity was the norm and the use of a bathing machine provided privacy.

Samuel Bayley introduced bathing machines to Bournemouth around the middle of the 19th century. They were in the charge of a woman attendant who ensured that the proprieties were observed and that the sexes were well separated when in the sea. A notice was placed near the ladies' area warning men not to come within 100 yards, and a 5/- fine was imposed on any who failed to keep their distance.

Sensible Condition
In 1903 the Corporation obtained from the Meyrick Estate a lease of the foreshore from Boscombe Chine to the Highcliff Hotel. There was one stipulation. An undercliff drive between the Piers had to be constructed within ten years and, if it was not done, all the land newly leased to the Council would have to be handed back to the Meyricks for them to develop as they wished. There had been objections to the building of the Undercliff by those who did not want to see their town change. This stipulation changed their minds and work on the Undercliff began in 1907.

Above Joseph's Steps in about 1890 can be seen amongst the wild ascent to the cliff top.

Above right The first zig zag at East Cliff.

opened – from the Pier to Meyrick Road – by Lady Meyrick. It was hoped that the success of this enterprise would change the mind of Clapcott Dean's heir, James Cooper Dean, to give similar permissions for the west of the pier. Gradually new sections were opened, and today it runs from Southbourne to Alum Chine and thence to Poole.

The construction of Undercliff Drive was typical of the improvements made by the town as a means of attracting visitors. Bournemouth was trying to shake off its image as a place principally to be enjoyed for its health rather than its pleasures. For a while, it was thought that *'visitors to Bournemouth are more shameless than at any other place'* – forcing a bye-law insisting that: *'Every female person above the age of 8 years shall, while bathing, wear a suitable costume or dress consisting of a tunic or blouse reaching from the neck to the knees with belt and knickerbocker drawers.'* The need for such propriety was hardly typical. Late Victorian Bournemouth was the pinnacle of moral respectability, and many writers and commentators thought it depressingly dull and tedious: *'dances and*

The Maze

Sometime in the second half of the 19th century, a 250 feet plantation with several pathways across it was known as the Maze. It was situated between West Cliff Road and the cliff edge. Once a feature of the locality, no trace of it remains today.

Visiting Party

A group of councillors visited other coastal resorts with similar cliff formations, including Ostend and Scheveningen. They returned in favour of providing 'a central rendezvous' to give a resting place for those walking from pier to pier. But that never happened, which explains why the stretch of promenade from pier to pier has no cafe.

The Livingstone Daisy

Mesembyanthemum is the little, green, cactus-like plant with a pink flower that still can be found on the cliffs. It was brought into this country by the Borough Engineer of the day, Mr. Lacey, after a visit to South Africa. He remembered how it had bound the sand on the Veldt there and wondered if it would be a solution for the problem in Bournemouth.

In the late 1970s the Beach and Cliffs Committee were told that the area had become a place of Special Scientific Interest (SSI) because the rare sand lizard lived there. This could be inconvenient, so the Committee went to search for it at one of their November meetings. They found none and were cheered. Much to their chagrin, they were told by scientific experts afterwards that the lizard hibernated during November and they had wasted their time.

Above Bournemouth from East Cliff in 1888 prior to the building of Undercliff Drive.

Left The Pier Approach and the Pier Head from the west in 1908, showing the completed first section of Undercliff Drive.

light concerts are discouraged', wrote one, 'and dissipation is said to take the shape of social bazaars and social meetings for charitable objects.'

By the turn of the century the beach was a place for families and the respectable young. The YMCA had a boathouse to the west of the pier, whilst those wanting tea or lemonade could easily buy both from one of the many stalls on the sand. Between the wars hawkers laden with hands of bananas wandered amongst the sunbathers: a good salesman could sell a ton and a half in a day. There was even a seller of dogs close to the entry to the Pleasure Gardens.

For children, there were pierrots and Punch and Judy shows, all adding

A view looking west over the flyover by the Pier Approach. The Hot Rocks Café, Court Royal, The South Wales Miners' Convalescent Home and the BIC are all shown.

to the sense of carnival that was Bournemouth in high summer. More recently, such attractions have been less able to meet their expenses, one factor in their gradual demise. Perhaps most regrettable is the case of Freddie Beale (1929-1996), who was forced to stop his Punch and Judy show because Bournemouth Council would not allow him a parking space for his 3-wheeler van near to the beach for unloading and loading.

The Pleasure Gardens

The Lower Pleasure Gardens, originally known as the Westover Pleasure Gardens, were laid out in the 1840s for the Tapps-Gervis-Meyrick family under the influence of Decimus Burton, and became town property in 1873. The Upper and Central Pleasure Gardens had been the property of the Durrant family. They were acquired by the town and laid out in 1871-89.

Originally, the Lower Pleasure Gardens were formed from about ten acres of rough fir trees lying alongside the Westover Road. Grass glades were planted, walks built, the brambles cleared, and the whole area enclosed with rustic fencing. A committee was formed to run them and residents were charged an annual fee to make use of them. In the summer, a band played in its Tea Gardens, drawing a large audience in fine weather. But much of the area was marsh, liable to flooding when there was a high tide, whilst the meadows above the bridge over the River Bourne in what is now the Square and the Upper Gardens, remained rough grazing land for cattle and horses. Drainage was eventually undertaken, and by 1873 formal gardens had been laid out and large villas had been built overlooking the stream, crossed by occasional wooden bridges. The draining had been a long and somewhat costly undertaking. Negotiations for public control commenced while the land was still in a boggy, undrained condition.

The Surveyor strongly urged the desirability of conveying the brook to the sea in pipes put underground, joined on to the sewer at the bridge, but this was not acted upon, and the Children's Corner has been handed down for the perpetual enjoyment of youngsters. A metal grid, still there after almost a hundred years, prevents model boats from drifting along the stream too far towards the sea.

The original fountain in the Pleasure Gardens.

Behind the band stand was the Invalids' Walk, renamed Pine Walk after the First World War in order to make the town seem less a refuge of only the unwell. It was once a great attraction. To the foot it was *'a dry brown carpet, formed by the fallen acicular leaves of the pine'*. Pine needles don't rot in the same way as deciduous leaves, providing *'a kind of felt carpet for the ground beneath'* after the autumnal rains. So *'invalids, who in other towns would fear to leave their rooms, may be found leisurely strolling along the dry carpet'*.

The Pleasure Gardens were then, as now, highly praised: *'the authorities have, by the resources of art, added in so great a measure to the beauty of their town'*. Electric light was added as early as 1899, and a feature from the 1930s-70s was a five-tiered waterfall over glass steps, backlit with coloured lights. It stood below the west side of the Pavilion but although a popular feature of the Gardens photographs of it are rare.

The rockery at the west of the Pavilion was delayed in its construction because building equipment left behind from the Pavilion had to be cleared, and the quarries supplying the necessary stone were flooded. Strangely, the Gardens were paid for by a loan from the Ministry of Health, which amounted to £13,700 repayable over 20 years. When the rockery was completed in 1930, it was one of the largest municipal rockeries in Britain.

A popular attraction held in the Gardens is the **Flowers by Candlelight** – 15,000 different coloured 'honey pot jars' with squat candles inside are hung on ornate fences to form pictures. The pots are lighted by 6,000 tapers issued by the Tourism Department to the thousands of children keen to repeat what their grandparents did before them. Back in 1896, the Princess Eugenie of Austria was staying in Bournemouth and a gardener hung a few hundred candles to cheer her way as she walked to the beach. The event is run by the Council every Wednesday night for six weeks during the peak summer season. The jars are specially made to withstand the heat of a burning candle. A commercial contract is awarded to a firm who check and renew them as necessary, tipping away any rain water which may have accumulated in them.

A Decoy Pond, further upstream, was so called because there was a 135 feet by 66 feet net spread out, inside which were a couple of tame ducks. Wild ducks were more easily attracted into the net for capture. This was

The Annual Summer Art Exhibition in the Pleasure Gardens parallel with Westover Road. Some of the paintings used to illustrate this book were bought from artists exhibiting here.

The Sculpture of Light hidden away in the Pleasure Gardens.

near the War Memorial and was then in the Parish of Holdenhurst. Coy Pond, further up the Gardens was not formed until the 1880s when soil there had been dug out for the construction of the railway.

The annual **Summer Art Exhibition** is a popular daytime feature held in the Gardens, parallel to Westover Road, and next to the Aviary. Some of the paintings illustrated in this book (albeit in black and white) were bought at this exhibition. Nearby is the **Aviary** which in 2003 was threatened with closure to assist in keeping down that year's Council Tax. After many protests in the local press, a private sponsor came forward to pay for its upkeep. In the same area is the hidden **Sculpture of Light** paid for by the Arts Council.

Bournemouth's 'Eye' is a tethered balloon with a 'basket' for about 20 people which rises 500 feet into the sky from the Gardens giving spectacular views of the town and the Purbecks. In Victorian times basket rides were as popular as they are today, often rising to 2000 feet at the end of an ordinary rope. The Eye uses nylon and steel, which is much more reassuring.

Westover Road, bordering the Pleasure Gardens, has always been a popular place. For nearly a century the pavement has been sheltered with a glazed canopy and older people called it 'The Bond Street of Bournemouth' and they regret it has changed.

Then came the big cinemas. The Regent, now the Odeon, with accommodation for 2,600 in one cinema, hosted occasional concerts including a memorable appearance by The Beatles. Two theatres and an Ice Rink along the road also formed the main entertainments of Bournemouth. The Ice Rink, privately owned and especially known for its popular ice show at Christmas and during the summer, closed in the 1980s; and the Palace Court Theatre, then the Playhouse, is now the Wessex Christian Centre. But, since the early 1990s, when the road was made one way, it has become a popular speed track for young people in their cars using the parallel Hinton Road as a continuous circuit. It is now a mecca for young people in the evenings at the weekends.

The Upper Pleasure Gardens towards Coy Pond were part of the Branksome Estate and a Miss Durrant allowed public access. A contemporary author wrote that the lawns were '*dinted by happy feet, and softening in their fall the sound of loving voices*'. It was also a happy playground '*for daisy-chain-loving children*'.

This account by Hadley Watkins is too splendid to be lost in the files of the local newspaper:

'*Start at the head of the Bourne and follow its course to the sea. As the area gradually widens the colour scheme becomes more and more enchanting, and on right and left from the houses on either side there are contributory schemes, which, from the greater height, must surely bear a resemblance to the wonderful Hanging Gardens of Babylon. Terrace upon terrace unfold new colour contrasts, and no one visiting Bournemouth during this season need heave a single sigh for that primeval garden which lay, if tradition be true, between the Tigris and the Euphrates. Those who have reason to know anything of Mesopotamia will agree that there*

One of the landmarks of the modern town is the Bournemouth 'Eye', which rises to 500 feet from its base in the Pleasure Gardens.

The mosaic designed by Maggie Howarth placed in The Square when it was pedestrianised in 1998.

is more of Paradise in Bournemouth . . . The business of the landscape gardener, as practised in Bournemouth, is surely one of the fine arts.'

The entries of **Bournemouth in Bloom** into competition have been outstandingly successful. Not only has it won 'Britain in Bloom', but 'Europe in Bloom' (*Entente Florale)* and the World Award. In addition to the gardens maintained by the local authority, there are various, keen, voluntary committees who maintain the flower baskets and flower pedestals in their areas, and colourful private gardens are appreciated by enthusiastic local residents.

Town Hall

The Commissioners held their first meetings in the Belle Vue Boarding House, though some called it an 'Hotel' – much to the annoyance of the Russell-Cotes family who owned the Bath Hotel nearby. In 1857, rooms were rented in the home of Christopher Creeke at Lainston Villa, near the Square and they met there until 1875, when they moved into a new purpose-built Town Hall (later converted into a shopping centre and now the Criterion Arcade). It could seat 700 people in its principal 40 feet high room, and was used for eleven years, after which meetings took place in the second Town Hall in Yelverton Road. Plans for a permanent building were drawn up to go to the west of the Triangle but these were rejected.

Finally, two acres were bought alongside Horseshoe Common to accommodate the construction of a new Town Hall, but within a few years the Council decided it was best as an open space. The Mont Dore Hotel was bought in 1919 and, after an expensive conversion, it was opened for

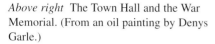

Above right The Town Hall and the War Memorial. (From an oil painting by Denys Garle.)

Above The Grand Hall which was attached to the east end of the present Town Hall. It was demolished in the late 1990s and replaced by additional local government administrative offices.

municipal purposes in 1921. The Council Chamber section was added in 1932. A Grand Hall was built at its east end and this was used for dancing, drama, dinners, school speech days, exhibitions and the Bournemouth Music Competitions Festival. It was a large, inexpensive general purpose hall for many to hire. In the 1980s it was pulled down and replaced by additional further administrative offices. Strangely, it was never really missed, as television had taken its toll of audiences for nearly every activity and the townsfolk expected a more cheerful building than the Grand Hall.

In 1974, the Town lost its County Borough status under Local Government re-organisation and became part of Dorset. A prominent Government Minister, Michael Heseltine, came to Bournemouth to explain to the Councillors in Room 10 what the benefits would be. Few of those present really agreed with this part of Government policy but, nevertheless, Bournemouth was taken out of Hampshire and those born in the town could no longer be described as Hampshire Hogs.

Education and Social Services' Headquarters were transferred to Dorchester, though small area offices remained. Police and Fire Services became part of the County. Then, nearly twenty years later, Unitary Status was granted to the town, and Education and Social Services were returned to Bournemouth. Offices were set up in Dorset House, Christchurch Road, for Education, and in Oxford Road for Social Services. Both were in rented properties. A thought was given to the purchase of the redundant hospital behind the Town Hall to contain them, but the capital sum for purchase and conversion was not available. It was easier for Local Government to pay out rent as revenue costs than to find large capital sums.

'I know why we are being put into Dorset', said one senior Councillor at the time of the town's removal from Hampshire, 'to help pay Dorset's bills. Hampshire has the wealth of Southampton, Portsmouth and Winchester. Dorset has only Sherborne, Dorchester and a few Piddling villages'.

THREE

Bournemouth at War

The First World War

The declaration of war on 4 August 1914 had an immediate impact on the finances of Bournemouth. There was a shortage of money in circulation. The banks closed for an extra three days after the Bank Holiday to enable the Government to print sufficient paper money so that they could call in all the gold sovereigns and half sovereigns.

All local foreigners – about 1,250, mostly hotel workers –- had to register at the Law Courts, and most had to leave the area. The effect on the tourist trade was disastrous until local women could be recruited into the industry to replace them. Most men had joined the Army. Anti-German feeling ran high. Mr. Wustenhagen, a member of the Municipal Orchestra since 1893 and who lived in the town with his non-German-speaking family, was forced to resign and leave Bournemouth.

The Crag Head Hotel on the East Cliff was turned into an emergency hospital and the Mont Dore Hotel, now the Town Hall, became a military hospital. During the first year of the war, 38 soldiers died in the military hospitals of Bournemouth.

The War Department scheduled Bournemouth as a garrison town for 10,000 troops. Initially, only 500 troops from the Hampshire Regiment arrived, leading to much disappointment from local families who hoped to

Music and a Scrub in the First World War
Rumours spread throughout Bournemouth as soon as war was declared in August 1914. Entertainments were to cease, and even the beach minstrels were told that barbed wire was to be put along the beach so they could no longer perform.

This led to a popular joke. 'Why would the Germans want to invade Bournemouth?' The answer was, 'Because they are a musical nation and would like to hear Dan Godfrey and his orchestra'.

Bands still entertained the somewhat reduced crowds and everyone sang the National Anthem with great fervour whenever it was played. The 16,000 troops billeted in the town were generously treated: the Laundry in Avon Road provided free hot baths for troops every Sunday morning, and 400 took advantage of this offer every week.

Indian wounded at Mont Dore
The hospital provided for 400 patients and staff, and was fitted with specially constructed slaughter houses to meet the need for different forms of slaughtering of animals. Indian closets, urinals, cook-houses, baths, and outside latrines for all the separate castes were needed, and these required specially adapted drainage. The outside latrine arrangements were constructed of 12 inch channels laid in a concrete and cement floor, partitioned off into 2'6" divisions. The channels were flushed by an automatic 100 gallon tank into a nine inch syphon trap at the outlet. This outlet was protected with an iron grating to intercept stones and cotton wool, the Indian toilet paper.

Animals were slaughtered to 'caste' methods in separate compartments, such as by beheading, disembowelling, cutting throat and bleeding. The flesh was cut up by special cooks for each caste as soon as the animal was killed. No apparatus, seat, fittings, or vessels of any kind were permitted by the caste regulations. At first sight such regulations may have appeared to be ludicrous, but after all, they were common sense, and were the best adapted for a tropical climate and race, where the prevalent diseases were mostly conveyed by filth.
Bournemouth's Chief Sanitary Inspector: Souvenir Book of the Royal Sanitary Institute 33rd Congress, held in Bournemouth in July 1922.

Bournemouth School postcard, Christmas 1917

This message was sent on a postcard by the headmaster and staff to all Old Boys of the School serving in the Forces:

'In spite of all our hopes the war has extended into a fourth year, and a fourth Christmas finds you still in arms against oppression. At this season, we, your friends at the School (Dr. Fenwick, the Masters and Boys) would like to be present in your thoughts, as you are in ours, and we send you this card with the assurance of our deep interest in, and close sympathy with you in the time of stress that you are facing with so much courage. We hope that our message may remind you of the happy days you spent here, and that their memory may help you to 'carry on' patiently and without complaint, until the achievement of that honourable peace for which you are so nobly striving.'

In 1939, the Mayor sent a Christmas card to every Bournemouth member of the Forces serving abroad.

Fampoux Gardens

Fampoux Gardens is the town's smallest public garden. It is at the junction of Green Road and Charminster Road and bounded by Firbank Road. It is a memorial to the Royal Hampshire Regiment (Bournemouth was in Hampshire until 1974) and commemorates the stand made by the Regiment at Fampoux in March 1918, during the Battle of Arras. The construction of the garden was done by unemployed servicemen.

Foundation Stone of the Holdenhurst Road Drill Hall

This stone was laid by Miss Georgiana Michell who generously presented this building to the Headquarter Companies of the 4th V. B. Hants Regt. Decr. 14, 1895.

– J.O. Vangelear, J. Roberts Thompson, Col. Creeke, Gifford & Oakley, Archts

On the inside walls of the drill hall were the 16 original stone tablets, protected by glass, which listed most of the officers, winners of the Best Shot Competitions and events of the local Volunteer and Territorial Units dating back to 1861. The building was bought for re-development in 2004 and the tablets were offered to the Royal Hampshire Regimental Museum who, regrettably, had to decline the offer as they had no space to store them. The local Council, however, will store them until a suitable place for them can be found. It is intended that the tablet bearing the name of 'Capt: C.C. Creeke, 1862' as a member of the 19th Hampshire Volunteer Corps, which was formed in Bournemouth, may be displayed in the Royal Hampshire Regiment Room at the Town Hall. The developers should be thanked for their efforts to preserve them and not throw them away as they so easily could have done.

offset the sudden wartime increase in the cost of food with their billeting allowance. As owner of the Royal Bath Hotel, a former mayor and leading citizen, Merton Russell-Cotes's influence was blamed for the failure of more troops to arrive, and he was forced to write to the local paper rebutting the accusation. But by November 1915, 16,000 troops were billeted, two or three to a house, in nearly every part of Bournemouth except for the central areas. The only ground for refusal was if no male lived in the house.

Kings Park became the town's main parade ground, and soon echoed to the stamp of boots and bellow of sergeant majors. Church halls were used to accommodate professional and amateur concert parties to keep the troops entertained. The pantomimes at the Hippodrome and at the Theatre Royal had 'House Full' boards out for every performance. The Concert Party shifted from Boscombe Pier to Boscombe Chine Gardens, in spite of the vicar of Boscombe St. John's protesting that it was unnecessary 'tomfoolery' in wartime. YMCA huts were provided at Winton and at Pokesdown and, later, in the Gardens by the Square. The Municipal Orchestra played on Bournemouth Pier to an audience of 5,000 at the Memorial Concert for Lord Kitchener, after he was drowned when HMS *Hampshire* struck a mine off Scapa Flow in 1916.

Paddle steamer trips came to an end and no boat was permitted to go out further than the Piers. The manager of the Royal Bath Hotel was fined £5 for permitting a light from one of the rooms to shine towards the sea. The Defence of the Realm Act of 1914, which prohibited the making of photographs or sketches within four miles of the coast from Hurst Castle to Lyme Regis without an official permit, was strictly enforced. A visitor was fined for carrying a camera at Pokesdown and another was fined for sketching in one of the Chines.

The Cloisters on the Promenade were used as the Wounded Soldiers' Rest Shelters and run by lady volunteers, supported by generous donations from the public. In the first 10 days of opening, 2,000 free teas were served, and, by their closure, 71,780. The Women's Emergency Corps was formed to cultivate gardens to grow food for families where the husband was in uniform and his wife working at an essential job to take his place. By the end of the war, 820 plots were being cultivated. Two National Food Kitchens were opened, one at St. Andrew's Hall, Shelbourne Road, the other at Peter's Hill, Winton. These supplied cheap, nutritious, hot meals for single parent mothers. In the first five months 173,573 meals were taken home.

The local Food Control Committee's contribution to the war effort was a poster in the Square spelling out the following message:

Bournemouth **Ob**viate **U**niversal **R**ationing **N**ow **E**very **M**orsel **O**mitted **U**ndermines **T**he **H**un. **F**or **O**nly **O**n **D**rastic **E**conomy **C**an **O**ur **N**ation **O**vercome **M**any **Y**ears **C**ontinual **A**nxiety. **M**uch **P**atriotism **A**lways **I**nspires **G**reat **N**ations. *Bournemouth Food Economy Campaign.*

The Second World War

On Sunday, 23 May, 1943 at around 1 p.m. 77 civilians and 131 servicemen were killed in central Bournemouth by enemy action. Beales, the Central Hotel, West's Cinema (now Burlington Arcade), all in the Old Christchurch Road area, and the Punshon Methodist Church on Richmond

Bomb damage May 1943. The Punshon Memorial Church and the Central Hotel, both on Richmond Hill, were so badly damaged they had to be demolished.

French Soldiers at Kinson School

'A few hundred French soldiers were billeted in the school at very short notice for three weeks during the Second World War. They slept on the floor in corridors, hall and classrooms. Four Moroccan soldiers refused to put down their guns, day or night, and slept with bayonets fixed, at the ready, with their backs to the wall. The soldiers took their water from the Kinson stream and also washed in it, making it run dry one morning.

When General De Gaulle visited the school, he asked to see the Headmistress, Miss Ward, to thank her personally, and gave her a special hug and kiss.'

Jean Budd in *A Gracious Lady* (The school was then on the Village Green at Kinson.)

Bombs on Bournemouth

November 1940, six parachute mines killed 53 and damaged 2,321 properties.

April 1941, four flats and Richmond Hill UR Church damaged. 8 killed.

May 1943, Hotel Metropole and Central Hotel damaged. 77 killed. Beale's store completely destroyed. Punshon Methodist Church destroyed.

Apocryphal?

The story goes that Hitler had announced his imminent invasion of England. It was his intention to hang every Mayor from a lamp post. There had always been a vast Conservative majority on the Council and therefore a Conservative Mayor, but J.J. Epsom, a Labour member, was elected to the office that year. Residents wondered why.

This villa at the Lansdowne was enlarged to become the Hotel Metropole which, in turn, was destroyed in the air raid of May 1943.

Dunkirk Evacuation

During the evacuation from Dunkirk in June 1940, many troops were brought to Bournemouth where they were accommodated in schools and church halls. French soldiers also came. One of Bournemouth's paddle streamers, the *Gracie Fields*, was sunk during the evacuation with the loss of 100 servicemen. It had been launched by the Red Funnel Co. in April 1936, the ceremony being performed by the stage star whose name she bore. This was the only local steamer to be sunk by enemy action during the Second World War.

Another local paddle steamer, the *Princess Elizabeth*, made four journeys to Dunkirk, rescuing 1,670 men.

Hill were all destroyed. The Metropole Hotel at the Lansdowne was devastated. Bombs fell over many areas of the town, damaging 3,481 buildings of which 40 had to be pulled down as they were unsafe. It was an attack by one bomber straddling its bombs.

The Concert marking the 50th Anniversary of the Bournemouth Symphony Orchestra took place two hours after the attack. It started with the National Anthem, and the Nimrod movement from Elgar's Enigma Variations was added in memory of those who had been killed.

Three months later, 1,455 properties were damaged mostly in the Talbot Woods/Winton and Springbourne/Shelbourne/Charminster Road areas.

Stokewood Road Baths and many church halls were used to accommodate bombed-out Bournemouth people, and additionally schools, Kinson Conservative Club, Kinson Liberal Club, the Labour Unity Hall, Redhill Bowls Pavilion and The Natural Science Society were used as rest centres.

Bournemouth became a 'Defence Area' during the Second World War, which meant that civilian visitors to the town were banned, civilian movement within the town was restricted and hotels and houses were requisitioned for government use. The US Army took over St. Alban's and St. Augustin's Halls, whilst the American Red Cross were at the Marsham Court and the Miramar Hotels. The Ambassador became a US Officers' Club, whilst the Carlton was used first as a coupon issue centre (for clothing and petrol) and later to house the American Forces of Investigation and crews of self-propelled guns. The Royal Canadian Air Force occupied The Royal Bath, Anglo-Swiss, Grand, Metropole and Linden Hall Hotels (the last three now no more). The Royal Pioneer Corps took over the Dunholm Manor Hotel as their Record Office, whilst the Royal Army Pay Corps occupied the Cottonwood Hotel. The Palace Court Hotel (now the Hilton) was said to have been a munitions factory, but this is perhaps doubtful, unless it was a highly specialised one in the basement or in the space now used as a car park, then the Majestic Garage.

Voluntary clubs, shelters and canteens were set up all over the town. The United Churches' Services Club was established at the Queen's Hotel, now Jacey House at the Lansdowne; it included a Chapel dedicated to St.

George of England. Many hotels accommodated clubs for use by the many service personnel in the town.

Within a few months of the outbreak of the Second World War, 2,876 children had been evacuated to Bournemouth, mostly from Southampton, and room had to be found for them in the local schools. Taunton School was sent to Bournemouth School; Portsmouth Grammar was accommodated at the College; and Tooting RC used the Temperance Hall in Haviland Road. Deanery Boys' School went to Alma Road School, and records show that school hours were 9 a.m. to 12.30 and 1.30 to 5 p.m., each school alternating the times for one week with the visitors. Wentworth (Milton Mount) School was also used. Education was often part-time because of logistics, but in less than a year of what became known as 'The Phoney War', nearly all the evacuee children had returned home and the schools reverted to full-time education.

After Dunkirk in 1940, French troops arrived, stayed at the College for a week, then 'vanished overnight' according to the Assistant Registrar of the College. Bournemouth School accommodated 1,500 soldiers, Bournemouth School for Girls had 800, and for a short time the pitch at Dean Court Football Ground was used for exhausted soldiers to sleep on. Expectant mothers and their children from Southampton, and also the College for the Association of Education Committees, which had been bombed out of their London premises, were later accommodated there.

Only after D-Day and the Normandy Landings could the town recapture some of its pre-war atmosphere. In 1944 the government cancelled travel restrictions for the August Bank Holiday weekend, and Bournemouth's beaches were crowded for the first time since 1939.

The Bournemouth Times on 8 December, 1944 reported officially released figures that between 3 July, 1940 and 29 February, 1944 fifty air raids had been made on Bournemouth.

One of Bournemouth's few Second World War relics, the air raid shelter in the Westover Gardens to the left of The Pavilion Theatre.

Casualties
Killed	219
Injured and detained in hospital	182
Injured	<u>325</u>
	726

Homeless Persons	401

Damage to Property
Totally destroyed	75
So badly damaged that demolition necessary	171
Seriously damaged but repairs possible	675
Slightly damaged	9,413
Glass broken only	3,256

During the war there were 988 alerts, 2271 bombs were dropped on Bournemouth, 168 civilians and 182 servicemen were killed, and 13,590 buildings were destroyed or damaged.

Three Victoria Cross Holders

The names of the three Bournemouth born holders of the Victoria Cross are commemorated on the scroll held by Lewis Tregonwell on the statue which stands outside the Bournemouth International Centre.

Three holders of the Victoria Cross were born in Bournemouth, and their names are commemorated on the statue of Tregonwell and Creeke outside the Bournemouth International Centre.

Corporal Cecil Reginald NOBLE was born on 4 June 1881. He lived at 175 Capstone Road and was educated at St. Clement's School and at The Art and Technical School. He joined the 2nd Battalion, The Rifle Brigade, and gained the VC at Neuve Chapelle on 14 March 1915 after cutting the wire when his battalion was pinned down by machine gun fire amidst barbed-wire entanglements. His mother received his posthumous award in November 1916. There is a memorial to him at St. Clement's School, and Noble Close in Wallisdown is named after him.

Sergeant Frederick Charles RIGGS lived in the same road as Cpl. Noble at number 39, though they went to different schools. Sgt. Riggs attended Malmesbury Park School, where there is a memorial to him. His name is also commemorated by Riggs Gardens, Wallisdown. Sgt. Riggs joined the 15th Hussars but transferred to the 6th Battalion, Yorks and Lancs Regiment. He won his VC at the Battle of Epinoy on 1st October 1918 whilst leading his platoon forward under heavy fire and capturing two German machine guns, which he then turned on the enemy: the posthumous award was made in January 1919. He also held the Military Medal for gallantry.

Lieutenant Colonel Derek Anthony SEAGRIM was born at 14 Charminster Road whilst his father was a Curate at St. Peter's Church, Bournemouth, 1901-04. He was commanding the 7th Battalion, The Green Howards, and won his VC in March 1943 during the Battle of the Mareth Line in Tunisia for leading his battalion into battle over an anti-tank ditch and attacking two machine-gun posts. He died on 6 April after being wounded at Wadi Akarit. Seagrim Road was named after him in 2002 and a member of his family was present with all the Colonel's medals, including the VC, for the naming ceremony.

His brother, Hugh Paul SEAGRIM, who was born in 1909, was posthumously awarded the George Cross in 1946. He was executed by the Japanese after voluntarily surrendering to them in an attempt to stop them torturing the Burmese villagers in the Karen Hills who were sheltering and assisting him avoid capture. After surrendering, in March 1944, he was taken to Rangoon and, with 8 others, was sentenced to death. He pleaded that only he should be executed, as the others had only obeyed his orders, but such was the devotion he had inspired that they all expressed their willingness to die with him and they were executed on 22 September 1944 in Rangoon.

Derek and Hugh Seagrim remain one of the most highly decorated brothers in British military history.

FOUR

Entertainments and Sport

The Winter Gardens

In 1873, the Winter Gardens Company purchased Cranborne Gardens from Robert Kerley who had used the land for archery, then fashionable. Four years later, and at a cost of more than £12,000, the great glazed building was opened, initially to provide a venue for a range of social activities and to be a commercial exhibition hall.

It was a financial disaster, even with a change of ownership in 1884. But it was a landmark building and the Council felt obliged to take it over and use it as a concert hall after extensive alterations were made. In 1876, Signor Bertini had brought his Royal Italian Band for one season and they stayed for sixteen, playing usually on the Pier. They wore military uniforms as all the players had been previous members of the Italian army.

In 1893, the Bournemouth Municipal Orchestra was formed under Dan Godfrey, the twenty-five-year-old son of the Bandmaster of the Grenadier Guards. It was the first permanent municipal orchestra in England, and Godfrey was soon made Musical Director and head of the Town's Entertainments. The Orchestra played amongst the hundreds of potted

Signor Bertini's Royal Italian Band
In 1892, the Corporation had just inaugurated daily concerts by this band. On Whit Monday, they attracted 24,425 on to the Pier, and continued to draw good attendances, proving financially successful by increasing the Pier receipts. Some inhabitants were not keen on the £40 a week expense while others raved about a 'horrid din' perpetrated by the band, though others marvelled at what was achieved with so little cash.
Bournemouth Observer & Chronicle, 1892.

The Winter Gardens in about 1900.

39

Dan Godfrey's Premier, May 1893

The great building was thronged with people. Never before has there been witnessed in Bournemouth such a gathering. The crowds continued to grow throughout the day, reaching bursting point at the evening's concert when its pavilion was packed so closely that locomotion was difficult. Wednesdays and Saturdays were highly popular evenings with many young people present. Ventriloquists and comedians appeared with the band, who would give a preview of a movement of the symphony that was to be played at the next concert. (sic)

Bedlam

At a public meeting in 1909, Mr. Maude, President of the Bournemouth Ratepayers' Association, said that the Winter Gardens was 'The most uncomfortable, wretched old greenhouse on the face of the earth'. (Laughter.) He had left a concert because of the draughts. To the few who said the Gardens were quite satisfactory he said, 'Then they ought to be in Bedlam'. The Town Clerk agreed with him.
Bournemouth Guardian 11 December, 1909.

Edward Elgar

Edward Elgar, egged on by Sir Dan Godfrey, had become a keen betting man. He was about to start conducting his Second Symphony at the Winter Gardens in 1912 when he was seen to pass a slip of paper to a messenger boy. A few moments before he stepped onto the podium, he was seen to hand Dan Godfrey some money. After the Symphony was over, someone heard that Elgar had won 25 shillings.

Winter Gardens Auction

on Thursday, June 9th, 1884, at The Mart, Bournemouth, at 3.30 p. m. for 4 o'clock.
'The Stately Palatial Structure is of glass and could fairly lay claim to the title of a Miniature Crystal Palace. It comprises a Quadrangular Building covering an area of upwards of 20,000 feet. The North Front is graced by a noble Portico, and smaller Vestibule Entrances are also provided in the East and West Wings. THE CONCERT HALL, with splendid pitch-pine flooring, is situated immediately under the magnificent Dome (about 70 feet high), and will seat 500 persons, the acoustic properties being excellent. The platform measures 29ft. by 25ft., and is prettily surrounded with Flower Beds. The Grounds . . . are varied and beautiful . . . with a Lawn Tennis Ground . . . and a SKATING RINK, 50ft. by 100ft., which is enclosed by a dwarf fence, the concrete flooring being faced with Portland cement, and accommodation also being provided for Lawn Tennis. In connection with the Rink are a Skate-House and Ladies' and Gentlemen's Cloakrooms. The READING ROOM is in the form of a horse-shoe, with seating all round . . . The GALLERIES measure 318ft . . .

plants that filled the Winter Gardens Palm House, which was, understandably, known as the 'hot house'. The chairs for the audience were on a flat floor and the platform for the orchestra was only about two feet high, which made it virtually impossible to see what was going on unless you were sitting in the front few rows. Although some alterations to the building were made, the Orchestra continued to play there until the Pavilion in Westover Road was opened for them in 1929. It was to be their new Concert Hall.

So the glass Winter Gardens, where Gustav Holst and Sir Edward Elgar had both conducted, reverted to the more humdrum life of an exhibition hall, as well as roller skating, boxing and similar entertainments. But the Council decided that its useful life was over. In the final week before its soaring glass panels were dismantled in the autumn of 1935, Sir (as he had then become) Dan Godfrey conducted a farewell concert, which finished with Haydyn's 'Farewell' Symphony, and ended with each musician in

Music

There is hardly a British composer of note who has not appeared as conductor of his own works . . . 35 British composers have contributed nearly 1,000 separate works. During the Summer Season, from May till October, the Municipal Orchestra plays each morning on Bournemouth Pier, and each evening at the Winter Gardens assisted by popular entertainers and vocalists. On Wednesday afternoons a Symphony Concert is given at the Winter Gardens and on other afternoons the Band is divided into sections for the Pier performances.
In addition to the Municipal Orchestra, the Corporation maintains a Military Band of 25 performers, which plays each morning (except Sunday) throughout the year on the Pier or in the Central Pleasure Gardens. On summer afternoons it plays in the various Pleasure Gardens of the Borough, and in the evenings on Bournemouth Pier.
Sir Dan Godfrey, Musical Director, 1922 Report.

turn stopping playing, blowing out a candle, and leaving the platform.

Once the old Winter Gardens had been demolished, it was replaced by a brick-built venue for indoor bowls. During the War it was requisitioned by the Air Ministry as a messing depot for the Canadian Air Force. Once it had been returned to the town, it was agreed that it should be converted into a concert hall for the Bournemouth Municipal Orchestra and renamed The Winter Gardens Concert Hall. On October 18th 1947 the Orchestra's new conductor, the Austrian Rudolf Schwarz, a survivor of Belsen, strode onto the platform amidst the sound of a prolonged ovation.

Despite the welcome, and a remarkable series of post-war concerts, the Orchestra's future was far from assured. Local people were proud of the orchestra, but did not support it in sufficient numbers to pay its costs – which seemed to increase almost monthly. In March 1954, a special meeting of the Council voted to disband the Bournemouth Municipal Orchestra on the grounds of cost to the ratepayers.

This action stimulated the formation of The Winter Gardens Society. They immediately raised £13,000, and persuaded the Council to pledge £37,000 a year to what was now the renamed Bournemouth Symphony Orchestra, who cracked off with a concert in October 1954 conducted by Sir Thomas Beecham. Sir Charles Groves became the permanent conductor, and it was he who spearheaded the increasingly popular tours the Orchestra made in the south-west of England and abroad.

Conductors came and went: Constantin Silvestri, Paavo Berglund, Uri Segal, Rudolf Barshai, Andrew Litton, Yakov Kreizberg, Marin Alsop. The young Simon Rattle, James Loughton and George Hurst were all assistant conductors; and the Orchestra won an increasingly high reputation for its musicianship. When the Poole Arts Centre, with its 1,500 seater concert hall opened in 1978, the Orchestra moved its headquarters there, playing only about a dozen concerts a year in Bournemouth. Hundreds of Bournemouthians say, 'They must return to Bournemouth.' But the Orchestra chose to go to Poole and to remain there.

As is usual with most local authorities, the repairs and renewals fund

Above left The interior of The Winter Gardens in about 1900. Notice the potted plants on the tiers behind the performance platform.

Above Sir Dan Godfrey.

Racist and Ignorant

The appointment of Rudolf Schwarz as Conductor of the Municipal Orchestra in 1947 was objected to by some members of the Chamber of Trade. Schwartz was an Austrian and we had just finished fighting them in the war. That he had spent years in a Belsen concentration camp was forgotten.

Some councillors spoke up. 'If you wanted a British conductor, nothing debarred Sir Henry Wood from applying', said one. But Sir Henry had been dead for three years. This was seized upon by the *Daily Express* and the town was held up to ridicule as being racist and ignorant.

'Beachcomber', an *Express* columnist, suggested that perhaps 'the Mayor himself could conduct the orchestra'. During his year of office in 1967, Mayor Crone conducted the Orchestra in the Radetsky March.

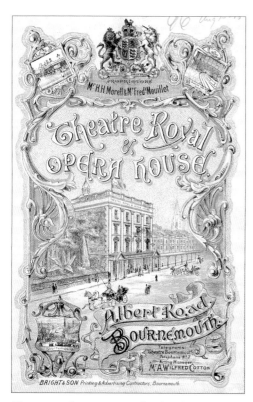

The cover of a programme for the Theatre Royal and Opera House, Albert Road, Bournemouth. (August, 1896.)

allocated to such buildings over the years has been inadequate to keep it up to date with the need for greater comfort, better air conditioning, more foyer space, modern box offices and improved back stage provision for artistes. Additionally, the entertainment industry has changed. The stars who toured or who did summer seasons now appear on television; and pop groups demand seating or standing capacities of 4,000 plus. The pattern of holiday making has radically altered and millions, instead of holidaying in their own country, go abroad.

Theatres and Amateur Dramatic Societies

There was only one place in Bournemouth where concerts and plays could be held before the building of the Town Hall in 1875, and that was at the Belle Vue Assembly Rooms, which stood on the site of the present Pavilion Theatre.

Bournemouth Amateur Dramatic Society appears to have been the first, founded in 1876. Sir Percy Shelley was their President and their first production was *The Dream at Sea* followed by the farce, *Turn Him Out*. The BADS *'continued their performances at the Town Hall for some years, with varying success'*.

The Bournemouth Lyric Club *'was a really first-class operatic society presenting such difficult productions as 'The Gondoliers', 'Dorothy', 'Yeomen of the Guard', 'Les Cloches de Corneville'* – the last of which was described at the time as the best amateur production *'seen on the stage in any town'*.

The largely amateur talent in the town was the driving force for a theatre to be built so that audiences could see professional productions. The end result was that Albert House, in what is now Yelverton Road (then Albert Road), was pulled down and replaced by the 800-seater Theatre Royal, which opened in December 1882 and was owned by Harry Nash, a theatre-loving stationer and printer who saw himself as a budding impresario. The local press commented: *'Blinded in his financial judgement by his hobby, careless that such an undertaking would have been regarded as none other than the work of some theatrical enthusiast.'*

The comment turned out to be reasonably accurate except for the support given to the D'Oyly Carte Company whenever it came, the packed house that greeted Oscar Wilde when he lectured there, and a reasonable audience for light comedies.

When the Town Hall opposite was turned into shops, Nash stripped his theatre and offered it as 'The New Town Hall' for balls, banquets and public meetings. Only a circus was popular, so it stayed six weeks. He converted it back into a proper theatre with seating for 1,100 and lost £5,000 in the 15 years he was there.

When the actor-manager Ben Greet played to nearly empty houses in the early years of the 20th century, he wrote to the press: *'I cannot think the Bournemouth public have deserted us, but it is a little annoying to find, when one tries something new and at great expense, they won't come to see it'*.

In 1896, two years after her husband had died, Mrs. Nash sold the theatre to a large firm of theatrical impresarios, but they seemed to fare little better. When the Theatre and Opera House in Albert Road was offered for auction on 5th September 1895, it was stated that it *'has comfortable seating for an audience of 1266, although the house is capable of holding 1,500 persons. The Auditorium, noted throughout the provinces for the ease with which the audience can distinguish the gestures, speech and songs of the performers, – and the Entrances comprise orchestra, 2 private stage boxes, spacious floor appropriate to stalls and pit, noble balcony, double gallery, 5 urinals, 2 w.c.'s, 2 lavatories, manager's office, pay box and vestibule. The Stage has a good rake, is 44 ft. wide and 22 ft. deep, and like the Auditorium is daylight if required. There are seven dressing rooms, property room, property stores, paint store, scene dock, lavatory, 2 w.c.'s and stoke hole'.*

During the Second World War it was used as a club for the Forces. It suffered fire damage in 1943, re-opening as the New Theatre Royal in 1949 for occasional use by amateur musical societies. In 1957 two local brothers who were professional opera singers opened it for operatic performances without much success. Then it became a cinema; then a bingo hall; then part of the Tatler Cinema Club. In the 1970s, pigeons used part of it as a roost and their droppings decorated the few balcony theatre seats that remained. Forty years later, the lower section is the Stanley Casino and the pigeons have been banished and replaced by a night club.

Archibald Beckett, who had built the Arcade at Boscombe, opened in 1895 the Boscombe Grand Pavilion Theatre which, ten years later, became known as the Hippodrome. By 1908 it had been enlarged to seat 2,000. It specialised in music hall entertainment and, because it was in a predominately working class area, it attracted good audiences. This annoyed a local vicar who wrote to the press: *'The variety shows will be damaging to my parishioners because they are not calculated to elevate taste'.* Yet they flocked to see Sarah Bernhardt appear in a French play speaking in French. But Beckett found that it was a struggle to find sufficient musicals and star-studded cast plays to attract big houses. Unlike many of Bournemouth's Victorian buildings, the Hippodrome has adapted to changing tastes. In recent years, it has been converted into a successful night club known as The Opera House.

The Bournemouth Little Theatre Club, an amateur group, built and owned for 40 years, was an intimate 565 seat theatre with balcony and stalls in Hinton Road. It was opened in 1931 as the Little Theatre and then became known as the Palace Court Theatre as it was almost attached to the hotel, now the Hilton. Ex- and prior-to-West End London shows often had runs there. The playwright Harold Pinter, acting under the name of David Barron, wrote his first plays when appearing with the Barry O'Brien professional Repertory Company, which played there for years to packed houses during the summer months. The amateur Club traditionally performed nine plays every season, but in the late 1960s the growing popularity of television resulted in shrinking audiences and the eventual sale of the theatre.

'The Gay Cadets' performed for many summers in a special 'theatre' on the West Beach and sometimes on the Pier.

Licence

The new owners of the Hippodrome, Morell and Monillot, applied for a liquor licence, as most of the audience flocked to nearby pubs during the intervals. The clergy said that it would be 'injurious to the moral welfare of both sexes'. Public meetings were held and slogans printed: 'Equality with Bournemouth'. The licence was obtained.

The Palace Court Theatre built by the Bournemouth Little Theatre Club in Hinton Road (1929). It is now the Wessex Christian Centre.

Amongst those to have acted at the Palace Court Theatre is the playwright Harold Pinter, who began to write his first play when performing there in weekly rep in the 1950s under the name of David Barron.

The Pavilion today.

In 1970, it was bought by Louis Michaels, who owned the Richmond Theatre and the Haymarket Theatre in London, and also the old J.J. Allen store where the Burlington Arcade is now. He spent about £100,000 rejuvenating the theatre but it was again not successful as a theatre or as a cinema. It is now the Wessex Christian Centre. Planning permission granted for its change of use still insists that the interior remains fitted out as the theatre it once was.

Despite the loss of its original home, the Bournemouth Little Theatre Club still flourishes in Jameson Road, Winton – one of the few amateur societies in the country to have its own premises. It seats an audience of 95 in theatre tip-up seats with each row raked so that there is a perfect view of the stage. Six different plays are presented each season. In 1964, the Club performed *The Tempest* in the open air on Brownsea Island, to celebrate the four hundredth anniversary of Shakespeare's birth. This in turn has now become the Brownsea Island Open Air Theatre, which presents Shakespeare to capacity audiences every summer.

There are many other amateur dramatic and musical societies in the area and the main Bournemouth ones are: Bournemouth and Boscombe Light Opera Company, who perform at the Pavilion to a large following; Bournemouth Operatic Society (Regent Theatre, Christchurch); Bournemouth Gilbert and Sullivan Society (Lighthouse, Poole); Bournemouth Shakespeare/St. Peter's Players; Kinson Community Association Players (Pelhams, Kinson); and All Saints Dramatic Society (at the splendid De La Salle Theatre, Southbourne.) The *Daily Echo* reviews each performance in the area, and runs the Curtain Call Awards, with an annual dinner at which certificates are given to winning participants in amateur theatre's many categories.

The Pavilion

No one doubts the importance of a Pavilion if a resort is to thrive, but the history of Bournemouth's is one of hopes raised and dashed, and a succession of schemes that foundered on cost, disagreement and the licensing laws. By 1900 it had become clear that the first necessity was the purchase of the 1¼ acre Belle Vue site, with its Hotel and Assembly Rooms. This was done in 1908, but the outbreak of war six years later brought about a halt. Progress finally restarted in 1922 with the announcement of a public competition for the building's design. Once the winner had been chosen, the Belle Vue site was cleared. In 1925 the foundation stone was laid, and a copper casket containing newspapers, coins, bank notes and other contemporary memoribilia was cemented in. The Pavilion was finally opened in 1929 by the Duke of Gloucester. Incorporating a theatre, a ballroom, three restaurants and two bars, its principal function was as a concert hall for the Bournemouth Municipal Orchestra. In due course a fly tower had to be added so that musicals and plays could be staged. Unfortunately, the repairs and renewals fund for the building granted by the Council was never sufficient to do more than repaint when necessary; so changes in the entertainment industry and the

Two artists' impressions of the interior of the Pavilion shortly before it opened in 1929.

The top view is of the Concert Hall: 'The provision of tip-up chairs, the installation of a ventilating system which propels purified air throughout the building, the delightful colouring and the elaborate stage settings, combine to provide that physical and mental satisfaction which is essential for the full enjoyment of the entertainment.'

The lower view of the Principal Dining Room, whose 'manager will be happy to furnish details and to suggest menus to those contemplating private dances, dinner parties or indeed any function which demands for success the resources of a fully equipped establishment and the services of a highly skilled staff.'

demands of modern audiences were hardly catered for. That has been the problem all along.

In 2003, the Council looked for a private firm to run it on a 99 year lease as it lacked the capital sum to bring the theatre into the 21st century and to clear the tatty external extensions to this Grade II listed building. Modern musicals are costly, and require complex technical facilities for handling scenery. It is the only lyric theatre in the conurbation able to stage large-scale musicals and opera, but audiences demand comfortable well-raked seating. Adequate multi-storey car parking for patrons needs to be close, as the Westover Road area is – perhaps wrongly – perceived to be young people's celebratory territory in which more elderly theatre goers tend to feel ill-at-ease.

All these problems will have to be confronted by the selected developer by about 2010, once the new casino has hopefully been built next to the Pavilion and the re-vamp of the BIC has been finished. It would be foolish if both the Pavilion and the BIC were closed for alterations and the Winter Gardens was in limbo.

The Pavilion Ballroom, with the fine sprung floor for dancing, is nostalgic 1930s; but the route to the toilets is like being in a public baths, hardly suitable for those wearing dinner jacket or evening dress. And this appears to be the only venue in the south of England which can cater for a sit-down dinner for more than 500 people.

Civic dignitaries would stand on the balcony of the Regent Cinema, now the Odeon, to take military and civic march pasts.

Cinemas

Edison's Electric Animated Pictures showed film of the Boer War in 1902 at the Grand Theatre, later the Hippodrome, Boscombe. By the First World War there was an abundance of local cinemas, all of them now closed. Their heyday was probably during the 1930s with the birth of the 'talkies' and again in the 1950s when colour became common. They flourished in a world without television and when few families owned cars.

The Picture House (The Savoy, Christchurch Road, Boscombe) was also a popular '*rendezvous for people who would take afternoon tea*' in the main vestibule, sitting in wicker chairs overlooking the street. A six piece orchestra accompanied the silent films. A Mr. Read remembered that the trumpeter in that orchestra became leader of that section in the Bournemouth Municipal Orchestra, so the standard was high. The relief pianist was Ernest Lush, who later became famous in BBC broadcasts.

There were other cinemas in the area: in Palmerston Road and another called the Clarence at the corner of Hannington Road. The Carlton and the Astoria were also at Boscombe. In Bournemouth were West's (Burlington Arcade) on the site of the Shaftesbury Hall, and once very popular; Electric (Poole Hill); Lansdowne Cinematograph Hall (197 Old Christchurch Road); the Bioscope (Bourne Avenue); the Roxy (Springbourne); the Palladium (Fisherman's Walk); the Grand (Westbourne), which had a retractable roof, 1000 seats, and served tea on retractable trays fixed to the seats, and is now used for bingo. The Moderne, the Ritz and the Continental (which showed what schoolboys a few generations ago deemed to be 'naughty' films and is now a pub known as the Hop and Kilderkin) were at Winton; and the tiny Premier News Theatre was in Albert Road. The Odeon at the Lansdowne has been used for bingo for years. And on Westover Road, the Gaumont, seating 2,000, which occasionally hosted musical stars, including the Beatles in 1964, is almost next to the ABC, both of which have now converted into multiplex cinemas.

Sport and Games

Dean Park Cricket Ground was originally laid out in 1869/70 on land owned by William Clapcott Dean. Sport first came to Bournemouth in the form of the cricket played by the Reverend Wanklyn's Pupils' XI on the meadows in the Upper Pleasure Gardens (the Pine Walk), and the Bournemouth Cricket Club, whose first ground was at Southbourne.

William Clapcott Dean was a cricket enthusiast, and probably offered the seven acre circular ground to the Club, with the result that by 1870 it had been returfed, and a pavilion, tennis courts, croquet lawn and bowling green had all been opened. The first match was in June 1871 between Bournemouth Cricket Club and officers of the Royal Artillery, since when the sound of ball and bat has been a regular part of the Bournemouth summer. Hampshire used to play there regularly, with occasional visits by touring Test sides. Today it is used by Bournemouth University and for occasional charity matches. Other local cricket teams play at Kings Park, Meyrick Park, Pelham's in Kinson and at the Electric Sports Ground.

Football is played today by dozens of clubs arranged in various leagues. The oldest is Bournemouth Football Club (known as The Poppies), formed in 1875 and with its own ground in Victoria Park. Junior-age leagues, now with 1,400 participants, play on Friday evenings and Saturday mornings at the Littledown Centre on synthetic turf. Organised Sunday morning games are also played by young children at Redhill with always about fifty spectators present.

AFC Bournemouth (known as The Cherries) is the professional football team which plays its home fixtures at Kings Park with a new stand built in 2002, known as the Fitness First Stadium. It attracts a gate of about 5,000 plus and has varying degrees of success in the Football League Divisions.

There are 16 local, municipal, open-air Bowling Clubs, and a privately-owned Indoor Bowling Club in Kings Park. Sea rowing takes place west of Bournemouth Pier from the Westover Rowing Club.

There are a large number of municipal tennis courts all over the town, and four private clubs. The West Hants Club in Talbot Woods is where the famous Hard Court Championships of Great Britain were held, and where the first ever pro/am tournament took place. Winners include Perry, Drobny, Mottram, Patty, Laver, Knight, Rosewall, Newcombe and Nastase. The ladies winners are equally illustrious: Dorothy Round, Doris Hart, Angela Mortimer, Christine Truman, Ann Jones, Margaret Court, Yvonne Goolagong and Bournemouth's own Virginia Wade. National tournaments are still played there and it boasts four covered courts in addition to 17 outside courts (10 clay, 5 artificial grass and 2 acrylic), a fitness centre and a leisure pool. It is owned by the Lawn Tennis Association and coaching for young people is regarded as a priority.

There are two 18 hole golf courses within the Borough: Meyrick Park, which has now been put on a long lease to a private firm who had the necessary capital to rebuild the club house; and Queen's Park. Both are highly regarded by the golfing fraternity.

Football

Football came to Dean Court in 1906 when Joseph Cooper Dean granted use of the land to Boscombe Club, the forerunner of today's AFC Bournemouth. In the 1920s, the team played in the Southern League and in 1923 it was elected to the Third Division South of the Football League.

The Club had started life in 1890 as Boscombe St. John's Lads' Institute FC. When it was known as Bournemouth and Boscombe Athletic Football Club Company, Ltd., it was the longest name in the League. George Parsley, a local man, was the first to sign professional terms.

Golf Course on Hengistbury Head

In 1911 there was a scheme to construct an 18 hole golf course on Hengistbury Head. This was the idea of the owner, Sir George Meyrick. It was hoped to attract 'a better class of golfer' – whatever that may mean. Membership was to be limited to 750, of whom 150 would be ladies. To ensure that only the most suitable players applied there was to be an annual subscription of five guineas. It was thought this would make the club exclusive. Life membership would cost £100. The committee was forced to abandon the idea.

Water Polo

Water Polo was born in Bournemouth. At one time, swimming at the end of the Pier was popular with the young men of the day, particularly on Sunday mornings. Some time in the 1870s the swimmers played around with a football in the water, and from this they devised a game and formed a team called the Bournemouth Handball Players.

The first competitive match was in 1876 when two teams of seven participated, but unfortunately the game was not finished as the ball burst. A week later another fixture was held and again the ball burst. However, the players seem to have overcome this problem as the matches continued.

It was from these games that the rules of Water Polo were drawn up.

Celebrations

The Royal Visit of The Prince of Wales in 1890

The Prince of Wales's first visit to Bournemouth was a private one when
he was only fifteen in 1856. With a night in the Bath Hotel and a walk
along the beach to Sandbanks, it was a much more modest affair than his
first formal visit to open the Westbourne Royal Victoria Hospital in Poole
Road, later the Eye Hospital until converted into flats in 2003.

By 1890 Bournemouth was self-confident and prosperous, and keen to
display its loyalty. Fourteen arches spanned the roads and a 100-feet-high
tower based on the Eiffel Tower was erected in the Square. Pies were
given away to the crowds in the Pleasure Gardens and the children who
lined up at Winton to cheer him on his way to Canford, where he was
staying with Lord Wimborne, were each given a bun. Canford provided an
even noisier welcome. 2,600 pheasants, 100 partridges, 30 hares and 120
rabbits fell to the guns at the shoot laid on specially for the prince.

The intended Grand Ball became a musical concert as the Royal Family
was in Court Mourning for the death of Empress Augusta. Lady
Wimborne stood in for the Princess of Wales who was unable to
accompany the Prince because of a slight cold, though some say she
refused to come because the Prince's mistress, Lily Langtry, lived in
Bournemouth in a house built for her by the Prince. The Princess's name,
however, appears on the Hospital's Commemorative Opening Stone.

And so it went on. Mayor Hankinson presided over a banquet for 500
at the Mont Dore Hotel where Dan Godfrey conducted the Band of the
Grenadier Guards. 360 members of the Hampshire Rifle Volunteers
assembled in Oxford Road and 230 Artillery Volunteers in Tregonwell
Road. The Dorset Yeomanry Cavalry marched to the County boundary,
then to Ensbury, where the Hampshire Carabiniers took over and marched
to the Winter Gardens.

Despite the lavishness of the welcome, it was noted that: '*In no place,
however, was the cheering of that very vociferous character to which their
Royal Highnesses are treated in other towns, but then, it must be
remembered, Bournemouth is essentially different from many other places,
and exhibits its loyalty in a more aristocratic and less uproarious – but
equally emphatic manner.*'

The visit wasn't a total success. One correspondent to the local paper
observed that, '*The Royal Visit to Poole cost a 4d rate but in Bournemouth
it was less than 1d. Yet Poole is generally reported to be poor,
Bournemouth to be wealthy.*'

Nor was the town immune to vandalism. Some Commissioners

complained that the illuminations on the Pier had been disappointing as, '*a number of boys and hobbledehoys blew out the lights, or candles were mischievously taken out.*' 1,100 lamps out of 20,000 had been destroyed.

Coronation of King Edward VII in 1902

Twelve years later the Prince of Wales became King Edward VII, and a spectacular programme of events was organised by the Council, with individual councillors in charge of every department. Nor were they above making a little profit on their own account. The Chairman of the Refreshment Committee, Alderman Stockey, was appointed one of the official 'Vendors and Refreshment Caterers'. Seven different bands played, usually two at the same time, but fortunately in different parts of Meyrick Park. There were miscellaneous races with prizes: the winner of the Plank Race for Ladies (with nine entries) won a £1.10s carriage clock. There were 18 entries in the 'V. C. Race for Men', for which competitors had '*to ride down course, pick up Dummy and bring back same*', and whose First Prize was a set of carvers in a case. Only two couples were bold enough to enter The Bisley Stakes Affinity Race: '*Lady and partner to ride down course hand-in-hand, dismount, break Three Bottles with Stones, mount, ride back hand-in-hand*'.

The Bournemouth Black and White Minstrels appeared twice and the Grand Illuminations had the gas for them supplied free by Bournemouth Gas and Water Co.. A Fireworks Display ended the eight hour long day of celebrations.

Bournemouth 1910 Centenary

The Centenary Celebrations were somewhat fraudulent. Although Lewis Tregonwell had bought land from Sir George Tapps a hundred years earlier, he had not built a house until 1812, at which point the town's history can more truly be said to have begun.

But the Council agreed to underwrite the ten-day-long celebrations with the enormous sum for those days of £30,000. They wanted to rival

The poster produced for the International Aviation Meeting, part of the 1910 Celebrations. South-bourne aerodrome was a grand title for what were open fields, as no other mention of an aerodrome there has been found.

49

Two of the banners presented to winners of competitions during the 1910 Centenary Celebrations. They each measure about 6 feet by 2 feet.

the celebrations held on the Riviera, whose Grand Grotesque Carnivals and a Battle of Confetti were regularly held in Nice. French experts were brought over to design some of the displays and floats, and one, the figure of Chantecler, was actually transported from the Continent, where it had won first prize at Nice.

Special Centenary Prix d'Honfleur Banners over six feet long were handpainted by Monsieur Giotti and awarded as prizes for vehicles parading in the Battle of Flowers. Fortunately the winners were asked to return them, where they now hang largely unnoticed in the Town Hall in the corridor to the left of Reception. They have been photographed for the first time to appear in this book.

King George V's Coronation, 1911

This was a memorable event for the children of the town. Bill Ransome, then a pupil at Alma School, remembers the day in June 1911:

'The coronation of King George V was one of the biggest events of school life, when 10,000 children, from all the schools in the town, took part in a gigantic Procession and Rally in Meyrick Park.

Each school represented a different country of the British Empire. Many photographs of this event still exist and a souvenir programme was issued with 85 photographs, all for four pence halfpenny. A number of postcards were printed of the procession passing the old Holy Trinity Church in Old Christchurch Road and of all the crowds in Meyrick Park.

Both my brother and I were in the Alma Road contingent which represented Canada and the West Indies. The lovely canopies of white material, with maple leaves carried by the younger section of the school, really took the public's eye and were very popular.'

Prince of Wales's Visit, 1927

After his arrival at the Central Station at 11.21, the Prince inspected five different guards of honour and viewed five different buildings before lunch at the Royal Bath Hotel at 1.13 pm.

Within an hour, he was listening to 8,000 schoolchildren, Scouts, Guides and Boys' Brigades sing 'Land of Hope and Glory' under Sir Dan Godfrey in Meyrick Park.

At 2.47 he visited the Disabled Sailors' and Soldiers' Workshop and the British Legion Hall in Winton, 'afterwards proceeding via Edgehill Road, Frederica Road, Talbot Road, Talbot Avenue and Wimborne Road to a Toc-H Ceremony of Light at St. Augustine's Church'.

He then spent three minutes at the Royal Victoria Hotel, Westbourne, before moving into Poole for three engagements and tea at the Branksome Towers Hotel.

He returned to London on the 5 p.m. train from Bournemouth West Station.

The Wartime Royal Visit of 1941

King George VI and Queen Elizabeth were the first reigning monarchs to visit the town, on 23 October 1941. It was supposed to be a secret, but hundreds turned out to watch airmen of the Commonwealth and Allied Forces march past their majesties along Westover Road.

Centenary Celebrations, 1990

By the end of these celebrations of the granting of the Charter in 1890, the Council had spent £180,000 which was called *'a scandalous waste of cash'* or *'a crowning achievement'*. The Press was waggish. *'At times the programme seemed destined to make a pretty good Ealing comedy script'*.

£70,000 went on the 'notorious' Boscombe fountain in the pedestrianised area which rarely seemed to work and when it did, green fungus grew down its white Portland stone where the water trickled. Letter writers to *The Echo* called for its demolition, but weary shoppers have become used to sitting on its slabs now the water has been stopped completely and a new incongruous Victorian style fountain has been installed.

The lasting monument of the celebrations is a Victorian cast-iron pergola in the Upper Gardens, on the left as the Town Hall is approached from the Square. It was constructed from several Victorian properties demolished along Christchurch Road, Boscombe, to make way for the Sovereign Shopping Centre.

Above left The Cock of the Day, 40 feet high, was brought from Italy (though some say from Nice, France) as a special attraction for the Parade of Floats held during the 1910 Centenary Celebrations. The figure behind it is of Cyrano de Bergerac. A tram follows pulled by hand.

Above Boscombe Fountain built for the 1990 celebrations in the pedestrianised area never seemed to work. This traditional fountain took its place within a short time.

Below The Victorian cast-iron Pergola in Bourne Avenue was erected in 1990.

The programme cover for the first Bournemouth International Festival.

These locally hand-carved goblets were presented to HM The Queen on her visit to the town in 2004.

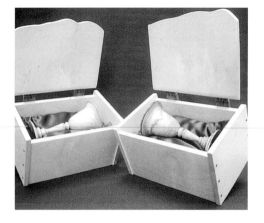

The Bournemouth International Festival, 1991

This Festival was launched with the confidence that it would, in time, rival those of Brighton and Bath. It was funded with a grant from the Council of £140,000 and £250,000 from commercial sponsorship, mostly in kind. It lasted for three weeks in June 1991.

The emphasis was on music, and nine world or UK premieres took place. Star names appeared: Sir Charles Groves, once the conductor of the Bournemouth Symphony Orchestra led with the Gala Concert, and Julian Lloyd Webber, Peter Donohoe, Tamas Vasary, Stefan Grappelli, Evelyn Glennie, The King's Singers and Andrew Lytton all appeared. Jazz enthusiasts were well satisfied with George Melly, Humphrey Littleton, Cleo Lane, Johnny Dankworth and Ronnie Scott. The Band of The Royal Hampshire Regiment opened the Festival with a Concert at the Pier Approach, followed by a firework display.

Five annual Festivals took place with different Directors, but out-of-town supporters, so vital for the success of any festival, failed to materialise in the numbers necessary. *'We would like more Fringe entertainments but there aren't any'*, said younger people. The hotels which might have hosted these Fringe events weren't interested as the holiday season had already started. Perhaps the accent of the Festival remained too much on serious music. But it was a brave try until money ran out.

HM The Queen and HRH The Duke of Edinburgh, 2004

Royal visits in the 21st century are relatively low key compared with the past. *The Echo* printed pages of arrangements beforehand but no thousands of children were organised to give 'displays'; no archway of flowers was built; and there was no grand luncheon or dinner for hundreds of dignitaries. *TS Phoebe* Sea Cadets, and the ACF 130 (Bournemouth) Squadron provided a guard of honour at King's Park for the Queen's opening of the extensions to the Athletics Stadium, which she had originally opened in 1966. The Queen and HRH The Duke of Edinburgh were provided with guards of honour by the Bournemouth Army Cadets and Combined Cadet Force when they went to Pier Approach, where they met 60 veterans of the Second World War. The Mayor in her speech said, *'I am especially pleased that the good work of many residents to improve things in Boscombe will be recognised by Her Majesty, as well as honouring a number of war veterans in this 60th anniversary year'*. The mention of Boscombe was because much was being done at the time to regenerate that part of the borough.

The Queen was presented with a 17" long stick of Bournemouth rock, made by a firm just over the town's border, and with two hand-carved, locally-made wooden goblets from trees in Boscombe Gardens. She then left for Poole to perform official duties there, including the opening of the new Royal National Lifeboat Institution College.

SIX
Servicing the Borough

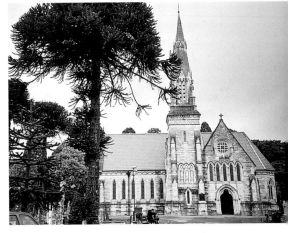

The Chapel designed by C.C. Creeke in the Wimborne Road Cemetery at 'Cemetery Junction'.

Cemeteries

The only burial place within the Commissioners' area of jurisdiction was St. Peter's Churchyard, which soon became full as Bournemouth's largely elderly population increased. Local people did not welcome additional land being made available for burial purposes, certainly not in the town; so the local Burial Board purchased 22 acres of land from William Clapcott Dean just outside the town's boundaries, at the junction of Charminster and Wimborne roads. The chapel in what became known as the Wimborne Road Cemetery was opened in 1878 and three different dignitaries of the three major denominations of the Christian churches performed their consecrations: Anglican on April 5, Non-Conformist on April 8, and Roman Catholic six years later!

The Boscombe (Gloucester Road) Cemetery was bought from Sir George Meyrick in 1894. Ludwig Loewy, the famous Jewish engineer, founder of Loewy Engineering, is buried here. The Northern Cemetery was opened in 1927. This also contains the Jewish Cemetery, and there is another cemetery for the Hebrew Congregation in the Broadway. The Crematorium was opened in 1938; before that, the one at Southampton had to be used.

A mortuary for people killed in the Second World War occupied the little hut-like building on the left along Castle Lane within 100 yards of Iford Roundabout. Until very recently it was a newsagent's shop.

Monkey Puzzle
An avenue of monkey puzzle trees in Bournemouth Cemetery was suggested to the Commissioners by one of its members, Joseph Cutler. The suggestion was accepted on condition that Mr. Cutler planted the trees at his own expense. Many were blown down in the great storms of the 1990s.

Early Snobbery
The 22 acres of land at Rush Corner were sold to the Commissioners for a burial ground at a nominal price by Clapcot Dean. The Chairman said, *'Mr Clapcot Dean had acted very handsomely'*. C.C. Creeke designed the chapel, whose foundation stone was laid in 1877. Naturally, Clapcot Dean was the obvious choice to lay it. But he was an ordinary 'Mister', so Sir George Meyrick performed the ceremony.

The Jewish Chapel in Kinson Cemetery.

Electricity

An exhibition of electric lighting took place at Dean Park Cricket Ground in 1878 and 3,000 people came to see it – a high percentage of the population. Perhaps they were attracted by the bicycle races and the football matches also arranged. But there were objections to the noise of the generators, and it was not until 1898 that the Bournemouth and Poole Electric Lighting Company were able to provide 3,000 lamps with sixty subscribers. This takes some believing. David Popham was cynical but realistic when he wrote, '*Like gas, power was generated at Bourne Valley, outside the Borough*'. The Council of the time were not prepared to have such an industry in the town. Parts of Kinson had no electric street lighting until the 1950s.

Fire Service

It was probably the serious fire in a large house on the site of the Sacred Heart Church in 1869 that led to the demand for Bournemouth to have its own, organised, Volunteer Fire Brigade. In the early days, riders on horseback had to be sent to Poole and to Christchurch for help, causing inevitable delays. But under Captain McWilliam, the town soon had its own second-hand, manual engine and equipment, all housed in the Corporation Yard in Norwich Road, ready for use, and a Code of Rules had been drawn up. Members were required to meet for practice on the first Friday of the month at 7 p.m. and fines were laid down for absence or disobedience.

It was decided that the Commissioners should be asked for '*a bell to give an alarm in case of fire, the arrangements at present for using one of the bells in St. Peter's Church tower not being satisfactory*'. Records of fires dealt with were not kept in those early days, but by 1885, the Volunteers took delivery of a Shand Mason Steam Engine. The Central Fire Station in Holdenhurst Road dates to 1902. It is now a student bar called the Old Fire Station, and what was the appliance room contains a frieze depicting various fire fighting scenes. Other stations were gradually provided at Winton (with a hose-cart park), Cromwell Road, Pokesdown, Seafield Road for Southbourne, West Hill Road, and Redhill.

There were 56 calls during 1906-7 and 111 new fire hydrants installed. Captain Lane of Bournemouth wrote an article for *Fire and Waters:*

'I am glad to say that, in my own town, it has always been looked upon as a respectable and gentlemanly thing to be a fireman, and I maintain that by self-respect of the community and by such means be the better able to do our work. Swearing is barred in our Brigade and I can claim that nobody is the worse for that.'

In his excellent and detailed book on *The Bournemouth Fire Brigade 1870-1929* Ted Hughes twice mentions occasions when different Mayoresses each broke a celebratory bottle of champagne against newly delivered engines. Would the scratch marks ever be removed? In 1923 in Meyrick Park, 2,000 came to see the first display of new turntables without horses. *'There followed the usual rather grand dinner with the town's chief officials as guests',* without which no ceremony in those days would have been complete.

The Volunteers came to an end in 1929 and the Fire Brigade became full-time professionals. But old loyalties linger on, and many former Volunteers continued offering help when serious fires broke out in the town.

Hospitals

It was natural in the early days that hospitals should abound, as doctors often recommended Bournemouth as a place to convalesce. Queen Victoria even told her Prime Minister, Benjamin Disraeli, to pay a visit to Bournemouth on the grounds of its 'very salubrious air'. As mentioned earlier, there was an Invalids' Walk in the Pleasure Gardens, and seven medical practitioners were elected to serve on the Municipal Council at the same time.

Bournemouth Public Dispensary opened in 1859 in Old Christchurch Road. Ten years later it shifted to a Dispensary Hospital with five beds in Madeira Road. Today's Stafford Road was once called Dispensary Road.

In 1874, 60 residents petitioned that it would be prejudicial to the interest of the inhabitants if a hospital was built in Shelley Road. After all, this was deep in the working class area of the town and the wealthy feared infection from what in those days were still described as the 'lower classes'. Nevertheless, it was built as the Boscombe Provident Infirmary, with a dispensary opposite Palmerston Road. It later extended in 1915 to a separate centre in Lowther Road which, in turn, became Avonbourne School and then the local Teachers' Centre.

There were strict rules for admission to the National Sanatorium behind the Town Hall. A patient could be admitted for each £5 collected in church, unless he could prevail upon a Governor to put forward his name. For a donation of £10, a child could be nominated to enter the Hospital for Hip Diseases in Children.

The Indian Hut
Early in the 19th century, smallpox broke out and a wattle and daub hut was built on land where the Five Ways Hotel is now. Those suffering from the disease were taken there and were left on their own. It was called the Indian Hut right up until the time the Hotel was built.

The Dispensary
Bournemouth Public Dispensary and Clinic opened in Old Christchurch Road in 1859. Ten years later, larger premises were built at Madeira Vale which then became known as Dispensary Road, now Stafford Road.

The undertaking was more properly a small hospital with accommodation for a few in-patients. The Dispensary served Bournemouth until the Royal Victoria Hospital in Boscombe was opened in 1874. No one was treated at the Dispensary if they earned more than £1 a week: the average weekly wage was much lower.

The first medical man to practise in Bournemouth was a Dr. Mainwaring who came in 1843.

The National Sanatorium opened in 1855. It became the Royal National Hospital and was converted into flats in 2004. Also shown in this engraving is the original Richmond Hill Congregational Church, built in 1859, which was demolished to make way for the present church of 1891.

The Herbert Home for convalescents in Branksome was founded by Salisbury Infirmary in 1867. Much of the equipment and planning for the wards was the work of Florence Nightingale.

As early as 1906, the local authority was trying to shake off the invalid image. The Medical Officer of Health advised that ambulances should be as much like private carriages as possible, so '*you can pass one in the street without distinguishing it.*' But within a year, 112 were to die from an outbreak of influenza; and the typhoid epidemic of 1936 was yet to come.

King's Park Community Hospital was originally known as Gloucester Road Isolation Hospital. When it was opened in 1886 it was said to be '*one of the best equipped in this or in any other country*'. Flowers were sent from the municipal gardens every day to cheer the patients. The large number of children's headstones in the nearby cemetery gives some idea as to the number of children who then died from infectious diseases.

As described in the last chapter, the Westbourne Royal Victoria Hospital was opened by the Prince of Wales in 1890.

The First World War demanded additional hospitals, albeit small, for the treatment of the increasingly large number of casualties being sent back to Britain from the battlefields of Flanders. Towns with appropriate accommodation on the south coast were especially required. The Mont Dore Hotel was the largest to be converted, whilst the St. John Ambulance

The Westbourne Royal Victoria Hospital in 1890. Later, it became Westbourne Eye Hospital. In 2003 it was converted into flats.

Brigade opened a hospital at 2 Bodorgan Road with 27 beds. By the end of the war two marquees had been placed in its garden. The Stourwood Auxiliary Hospital at 3 Bracken Road, Southbourne, gradually extended to care for 52 wounded soldiers, whilst the Crag Head (Hotel) Red Cross Hospital in Manor Road dealt with acute cases.

As we live longer, the demand for 'nursing homes' increases. Bournemouth still has a stock of Victorian and Edwardian houses large enough to be converted for this purpose. However, modern Health and Safety legislation often demands expensive modifications. The requirement for flats and their subsequent rise in price has made it more financially advantageous for nursing home owners to sell their properties to developers who, once planning permission has been obtained, are able to convert or demolish the buildings for flats. This has led to a shortage of accommodation for the elderly.

The most serious crisis in Bournemouth's medical history was undoubtedly the **Typhoid Epidemic of 1936**, which broke out before antibiotics had been discovered. By 20 August, 315 people had visited their doctors with similar symptoms. The next day, a Ministry of Health doctor from London arrived, and within 24 hours he had established that Frowds Dairy in Poole was the common factor. That very day, the dairy began pasteurising its milk, thus preventing further infection. Additional doctors and nurses from outside the area were called in and temporary huts were hastily built to accommodate the patients.

In those days pasteurisation was not legally required, nor was it popular with most people. The contamination had entered the milk supply of a small local farm in Dorset who sent 20 gallons of milk a day to the central dairy who mixed it with 1,600 gallons of milk which came from 37 other herds.

And 10,000 customers had received the contaminated supply just before the August Bank Holiday. This scared both the holiday trade and the Council, so the seriousness of the situation was deliberately played down so visitors should not be put off from holidaying in the town. The tourist trade was vital for the local economy. Local papers did not mention typhoid, and typical headlines were: 'Infected milk — no cause for anxiety'.

The mug issued in January 1890 to commemorate the opening of the Royal Victoria Hospital, Poole Road, Bournemouth by The Prince of Wales.

But 51 people died, many of whom were children.

A national newspaper criticised the decision for not giving '*day to day exact details of the fresh cases and of the steps being taken to control them. Then rumour would have been killed and Bournemouth's reputation for honesty, at any rate, would not have suffered*'. The Chief Officer at the Ministry of Health made this general comment: '*The population at risk is greatly increased by the modern trend to concentrate a large part of the retail in one combination . . . A single contributory farm may be catastrophic in its results . . . In the present state of our knowledge . . . the only way to reduce the risks of such outbreaks to a minimum is by pasteurisation.*' The financial effect of the epidemic was noticeable. It cost the Council £23,000 which had to be raised from loans. Traders agreed not to press for overdue payments from local people.

A Public Inquiry was held *in camera* at Bournemouth Town Hall in February, 1937. The Chairman of Bournemouth's Health Committee, Cllr Dr Asten, said '*he thought Judge Cotes-Preedy's Report was a happy ending to the affair*'.

The main Royal Victorian Hospital was in Shelley Road, Boscombe, and was developed into flats as soon as the striking blue-roofed Royal Bournemouth Hospital with 668 beds was opened by the Princess Royal in Castle Lane in November 1990.

Police

The first police officer in Bournemouth was recorded in 1856, but it was thirteen years before a Police Station was built in Madeira Road, where the present main station is situated.

Mate and Riddle report: '*It occurs to us that here was a golden opportunity for any evilly-disposed person to carefully prepare his plans, take advantage of the policeman's night off – and make a good haul. Indeed, something of the kind occurred . . . and the Chief Constable was asked if he would allow a constable to be permanently attached to the place during the night.*'

Prior to 1856, trials were at Ringwood Petty Sessions; then they were held at Christchurch.

In 1879, additional police were drafted in for the November 5th celebrations, '*taking their uniform with them in a carpet bag . . . so as to disguise their being PCs. On arriving at Bournemouth they will walk quietly to the Police Station . . . one pint of beer only to be given previous to going on duty*'.

By 1892, there were 44 officers and a Superintendent. The town had its own Constabulary by 1948, but with Local Government Reorganisation in 1974, it became part of Dorset County Police, and it still is.

Today, there are Police Stations at Winton, Boscombe and Kinson. In 2002, the Police Authority wished to build a new Station partially on the Village Green at Kinson, but the local councillors mounted such a protest that the idea was scotched. There is now a police 'shop' on the main road.

Bournemouth Police Station, Madeira Road.

The Post

The first post office was at the Tregonwell Arms a year before the penny post began in 1840. A postman from Poole advertised that he would 'deliver and receive the Post Letters at Parkstone, Bourne and the Immediate Neighbourhood, and call at the Bath Hotel and the Tregonwell Arms every day'. The main Bournemouth Post Office by 1878 had a staff of two, and there was an Inspector and six postmen, but only ten pillar and wall boxes. Thirty years later, the postal staff numbered 404, and for many years the post office opened for fourteen hours a day, Sundays excluded.

Sadly, extensive enquiries in 2005 have been unable to reveal comparable figures.

Above The Tregonwell Arms served as the first Post Office. It was demolished in 1885, allowing the *Bournemouth Observer and Chronicle* to indulge in a moment's nostalgia: '*Though not an ancient historical building it has been regarded locally with a kind of veneration, partly from the fact that it is one of the oldest houses in Bourne-mouth, and partly because its retired position and ivy-mantled porch gave it an air of a respectable old age. . . We were not altogether surprised to see persons cutting slips and leaves from the ivy as relics of the old house.*'

Below Bournemouth's Victorian post box on the East Cliff.

Communications

As early as 1867 an electric telegraph linked to Poole and thence to London was available at moderate charges for transmissions of messages from Mr. Rebbeck's estate agent's office at the foot of Old Christchurch Road, known as Rebbeck's Corner. His son, Edward, known as 'Colonel', became Mayor in 1891.

The first known receiving box for letters appears to have been at Mr. Sydenham's Reading Rooms next to the Belle Vue near the sea by the Lower Pleasure Gardens.

A Hairdresser

'*Mr. W. Attwell, hair cutter and dresser, of Christchurch, attends at Bournemouth every Tuesday and Friday, and orders for his services might be left at the Post Office or at the Tregonwell Arms.*'
Bournemouth Directory, 1860.

Water and Gas

Water and Gas were lumped together because the Commissioners thought they should be, so Bournemouth lagged behind London by fifty years in the provision of gas lighting – 1864. Surprisingly, the demand for it was slow until it was reduced in price. Then, the Bournemouth Gas and Water Company joined with the Poole Gas Company in 1903 and was thus able to obtain coal more cheaply because it was landed by ship at Poole Quay, which was cheaper than bringing it in by rail. Gas was nationalised in 1949.

Water at first was obtained from brooks and springs in Bourne Valley. Later a well 60 feet deep was sunk in the gravel nearby. As demand grew, more water was obtained from the gravel beds at Longham by the River Stour. When additional supplies for a growing population were required, a bore hole 200 feet deep through the chalk was sunk at Walsford near Wimborne, and was piped to Alderney and then into the town by gravitation. Because the water from this source was very hard, the largest water softening plant in the country was installed. As demand grew, supplies came from near Crichel and the chalk aquifer of Cranborne Chase.

Above Gas lamps were hung over the centre of the road in many parts of the town and maintained with disregard for today's Health and Safety regulations.

Right Palmerston Road Water Tower.

> ### Gas Lighting
> Gas lighting was introduced to Bournemouth in 1864; 50 years after London. Its supply had been offered to the Commissioners, but they would not contemplate a scheme unless it provided for the supply of water as well. A plan was submitted by a Mr. Bennett in 1861, but it was turned down by the Commissioners on the grounds that they had insufficient funds to provide lighting in the streets. A year later, the Bournemouth Gas and Water Company was established and, at last, both water and gas could be supplied by the same company.
>
> An electricity generator near Dean Park was closed down because it made too much of a hum for residents nearby.

Water Towers

There are/were four impressive water towers in the town and all are of great architectural merit. The one in Palmerston Road, Boscombe, holding 160,000 gallons, was built in 1875 to help with the supply of water for Springbourne and Boscombe. The Water Tower in the Upper Pleasure Gardens, built ten years later, was fed by a water wheel. It powered sprinklers for the gardens and assisted with the relief of the flooding there. It also supplied the fountain which was on an island in the stream nearby, but was removed in 1991. Its design was based on a medieval castle and it is now home to protected bats.

The first ferro-concrete water tower in the country was built in 1900 for the Borough Council in Meyrick Park near the club house of the golf course. Unfortunately it was deemed to be unsafe and was demolished in the mid-1990s.

The Water Tower in Seafield Road, Southbourne, was built in 1875 to aid the supply of water to Southbourne-on-Sea and it was connected to the 'Russian' waterworks in Iford Lane. The water from the river was rather unclean so the supply was taken from the mains. It is a listed building and now houses aerial masts for mobile phone coverage.

The water tower in the Upper Pleasure Gardens.

Transport

The Municipal Tramways

Arguments and delays, but not unforeseen heavy costs, were only to be expected before the first Bournemouth tram made its journey in May 1902 on a line from Pokesdown to the Lansdowne. It was argued that tramways might be convenient for some, but the roads were too narrow; trams were too noisy; and to have an outside company providing the service, the British Electric Traction Company, would not be welcome. But the BETC was tenacious and promoted a Bill in Parliament to run a line from Christchurch to the Lansdowne and other lines within the Borough. The Council was instructed that it had to complete the line it had planned itself within two years. It had already spent £200,000 doing the planning, yet refused to enter into an agreement; so the BEC took the Council to Court. Claims and counter claims nearly went as far as the House of Lords. It all cost the Council an extra £112,000, a vast sum in those days. But before long a network was built, the bridge at Tuckton was constructed and, by 1906, most of the main parts of the town had a tram service, and lines were gradually extended to Christchurch and to link up with the Poole service to County Gates which ran there in 1901.

Overhead lines were used except for 2¾ miles through the town centre, where the power was obtained from rails in the road (conduits), so that ugly lines and poles would not be seen; but these were replaced in 1911. The tram depots were at Southcote Road, which still exists; next to the Bell Inn at Pokesdown there was a large turntable for trams and, later,

Bournemouth Corporation Tramways, 1907. Number of Passengers:

Thur 10 Jan	37,488
Fri 11 Jan	33,867
Sat 12 Jan	39,480
Sun 13 Jan	4,924,
Mon 14 Jan	34,198
Tue 15 Jan	33,461
Wed 16 Jan	35,559.
Weekly total	218,937

Tram 27 on its way to Winton.

trolley buses, which existed until the 1960s (now flats); and there was another at Moordown (now a supermarket).

No 1. Tram was the Mayor's Tram, and it inaugurated the service accompanied by much flag-waving and an obligatory, celebratory tea. This tram could be used for private hire . . . and it ended its days as a bus shelter at Iford.

On May 1st 1908 the country's worst accident in tram history happened where 'the pagoda' at the rear of Marks and Spencer, Bournemouth, is now. The brakes of Tram No. 73 failed as it descended the incline of Avenue Road and it overturned and fell into the garden of Fairlight Glen. Seven people were killed and 26 people were injured. The average speed of a tram was 8 to 10 m.p.h., and at the Inquiry it was suggested that the tram reached about 70 m.p.h. before it crashed; but this speed is difficult to believe. In 1932, a motor bus went out of control at Boscombe Pier and

The Mayor's Tram, No 1, ended its days as a bus shelter at Iford.

Public Clocks

These were regarded as necessities in the days before the ordinary person carried a watch. Bournemouth had four. The first, presented in 1882 by the local MP, Horace Davey, was at Bournemouth Pier. The casing which encircled the clock can now be seen on top of the James Fisher Medical Centre off Castle Lane.

The four-sided clock in the Square, which used to be over the tram shelter and then on a tower, was presented by Capt. Harry Norton, JP in 1925. Three sides remain; the fourth acts as the Camera Obscura above the cafe recently built there. Norton had a road in Winton named after him.

There is another public clock on the tower of East Cliff United Reformed Church, which was once kept a minute fast for the convenience of travellers catching a train at the railway station opposite. It was recently restored at a cost of £60,000.

The face of the clock on the Municipal College at the Lansdowne dates from 1913. The clock was presented by the mother of another of the town's MPs, Mrs. Croft. It used to strike only between 7 a.m. and 10 p.m. and, because it had no numbers on its face, it was called Mate's Folly after the then Mayor.

There was a public clock on the now demolished Holy Trinity Church.

Charabanc Trips

In the days when fewer people owned cars, charabanc trips were the popular method of transport for going on 'outings'.

Charabancs were long, open vehicles with rows of transverse seats and a canvas hood. In the early days, the tyres were solid, not pneumatic.

Charabancs were parked all round the Square with the drivers touting for business. The favourite trip was a day tour to Cheddar to view the caves and then on to Wells to see the cathedral. This cost 12/-. The tour left at about eight in the morning and passengers who pre-booked would be picked up by taxi at their homes at no extra charge.

When the *Queen Mary* was in dock at Southampton, trips were arranged for visitors to have a tour of the ship.

Tram Clocks
Christchurch Road, Boscombe, from the
Arcade to Ashley Road, was not as wide as it
is today, and had a double set of tramlines
running down the centre, so passengers had
no option when getting on or off but to cross
the road to and from the pavement. The road
itself, right through from Pokesdown to
Bournemouth, consisted of tarred wooden
blocks. There was a series of special clocks
on the route. The driver would turn a key and
ring a bell to record the time he was at each
clock.

Right A Corporation trolley bus. The service
from the Square to Westbourne started in 1933,
and by New Year's Day 1936 the entire network
from Cross Roads to County Gates was in
operation.

crashed into the sands, killing two people.

There was no Sunday service, which made it difficult for hotel workers living in the outer areas to get to work in the central hotels, and the service began (though only in the afternoons) after a vote was taken at the Local Elections in 1912. That decision remained in force until 1926.

The famous double-decker, electric trolley bus service, the envy of the whole country, began on an experimental basis in 1933 and lasted until 1969. It was popular and silent, but there were two disadvantages: occasionally the two arms sprouting from its roof would become detached from the overhead wires and the bus conductor would have to slide out a 20 feet long pole from under the bus to put them back again, much to the cheering of the local children. Perhaps, more importantly, operating costs became prohibitive and spare parts difficult to obtain. So motor buses were phased in and the last trolley made a nostalgic journey from the Pier to Christchurch Priory, with large crowds cheering it on its way as it returned to the depot at Mallard Road, off Castle Lane. This depot became a listed building in 2001, causing development problems when the Transport Bus Depot shifted to new premises behind the Castlepoint Centre in Yeomans Road in 2004.

Below A circular tour of the town and the
surrounding area accompanied the clinking
delivery of milk. Note the early 'EL' letters of a
Bournemouth number plate.

Below right The Bus Station in the Square on
the site of Lainston Villa.

The Cliff Lifts

These should be known as funicular railways. There are three. The one on the East Cliff was opened in April 1908. Lady Meyrick refused to attend if she would have to ride in it, even though her husband, George, was performing the opening ceremony. 'It's a dangerous contraption', she claimed. The track is 52 metres long rising up the 36 metre cliff at an angle of 45°. Two cars each run on a 5'6" gauge track originally supported on timber but replaced with precast concrete in 1986. The 500 volt DC supply has been changed to a 3 phase 415 volt AC supply. Twelve passengers can be carried in each car, and during the peak holiday seasons about 20,000 passengers a month use the facility.

The West Cliff Lift (August 1908) carries 16 passengers; the one at Fisherman's Walk was built by the direct labour force of the Council under the Borough Engineer, Mr. F.P. Dolomore, who personally opened it in 1935. To quote from the town's publicity: *The lift speeds have been reduced to less than 0.05 mtrs/sec to ensure users a sedate ride and a smooth stop.*

Railways

When the first railway in the area was opened in 1847, Bournemouth was missed because it hardly existed – just a few houses. The line went from Southampton to Brockenhurst, then to Ringwood and then on to Wimborne, Wareham and Dorchester. The line from Poole to Southampton was known as Castleman's Corkscrew because of the circuitous route it took to avoid Bournemouth.

The early residents of Bournemouth were not keen on trains for fear they might bring 'trippers', who were perceived as mostly being working class. What was worse, ran the argument, if they came on a Sunday, it

The East Cliff Lift carrying Sir George Meyrick on its 1908 opening day. In those days it was known as a Car Lift. Note the crowds gathered for the ceremony.

Lunch Breaks

A few decades ago, the lifts would be shut at lunchtime and many would-be users complained. The Council stopped the lifts because of the cost. At that time, the drivers were members of the National Union of Railwaymen and Union rules insisted on a lunch break, which meant employing another driver for each of the lifts for an hour.

The construction of the railway line, Holdenhurst Road. St Paul's Church and the chimney of the Bournemouth Brewery (both now demolished) may be seen in the background.

65

Right Bournemouth Central Railway Station, showing its 'winter garden' interior in 1911. The station is now a listed building, delaying repairs after damage by storms. British Rail wanted to demolish and rebuild, and controversy raged.

The single span over the 350 feet long platform measures 95 feet and is 45 high. The roof is supported by twelve girders, each weighing nearly 18 tons.

Russell-Cotes and Trains

Merton Russell-Cotes objected to Sunday trains unless there was only one for doctors and others visiting their sick relations. He said, *'Bournemouth is a sanatorium, and the majority of visitors come to get quietness and immunity from vulgar crowds'.*
The Commissioners voted 7 to 4 to agree.

Unwanted Trade

The town catered primarily for the wealthy until the coming of the railway. With a journey time from London of only three hours, thousands then started coming as day-trippers, lowering the tone. Finally, the Council was prevailed upon to make an official request to the railway company that cheap day-tickets should not be issued after 31st July each year. The railway company refused the request – fortunately for Bournemouth.

In 1890 4,000 people came down from Birmingham on a one-day excursion. Two hundred missed the last train back, so a special train was laid on for them!

---

would *'necessitate the opening of public houses and refreshment places that would interfere with the quietness of the Sabbath which would not be at all conducive to the best interests of the town'.*

Thus travellers who wanted to come by rail to Bournemouth had to catch a horse-drawn carriage from the stations at Holmesley, Christchurch, or at Hamworthy, Poole, where there was a service to the Bath Hotel.

By the 1860s financial commonsense prevailed over middle-class morality. Discussions began about the best route for Bournemouth to be joined to existing lines. West Moors, which joined to Salisbury, found favour. The journey from Salisbury to London took only 2½ hours, compared with 4 hours from Ringwood. Landowners on this route were not keen, and the promoters missed the chance for a Bill to be introduced to Parliament in that session. A route which would go through Meyrick Park (then known as Poors Common) was objected to and so was a line and station in Branksome Wood Road. At least a dozen public meetings were held over the issue, including one which was attended by 700 people, a high percentage of the population of the time.

Negotiations continued with the London and South Western Railway and, by 1870, a line had been constructed from Christchurch to Holden-hurst Road as the terminus of a single line section of the Ringwood, Christchurch and Bournemouth Railway. The small terminus was a single platform on the east side of Holdenhurst Road, and in due course this became Bournemouth East Station. Four years later, another line was opened from Poole, arriving at Bournemouth West. Following the construction of Bournemouth Central on the west side of Holdenhurst Road (the present Bournemouth Station), the two stations were finally linked in 1888. Pokesdown Station was opened (much to local protest) in 1886, and was originally known as Boscombe Station.

A letter from Merton Russell-Cotes published in the *Bournemouth Observer* perhaps explains why Bournemouth stations were so far from the town centre.

'I do not think there is the slightest need to alter the positions of the east and west stations: on the contrary, I think it an immense boon to the place, and one of its greatest charms, that we have no engines whistling in our midst, and wise counsels prevailed when it was decided to keep the termini

The railway bridge and the nearby Halt over Meyrick Park that closed in 1917.

Bournemouth Belle

The Bournemouth Belle Pullman Train ran between Bournemouth and Waterloo in just over two hours. A small supplementary charge was made and passengers were provided with armchairs and tables. The accent was on elegance, with lamps on the tables and lavish décor. All baggage was carried in the luggage van, and no cases were allowed in the carriages. The service began in July 1931 and continued until the outbreak of War. It resumed in 1946 but was withdrawn in 1967.

Dog Carts

The use of dogs as draught animals was not an unusual sight in Bournemouth, as the Poole fishermen brought their catch in small carts drawn by dogs. The carts were about 3ft x 2ft x 1ft. In 1849 the use of dogs for such purposes was made illegal, but the fishermen carried on using them until St. Barbe Tregonwell, son of Lewis Tregonwell, placed himself at the top of Commercial Road (then Poole Road) and stopped the fishermen bringing their carts any further.

so far removed into the suburbs . . . If, however, the Company must have a central station, there is only one position in Bournemouth for it, namely Dean Park.'

He also advocated that there should be only one Sunday train as those who came to the town on that day should be doctors and relatives visiting the sick. *'Bournemouth is a sanatorium,'* he argued, *'and the majority of those who (have come) to the town want quietness and immunity from vulgar crowds.'*

The steam motor car had been designed to run on railway lines by the Chief Engineer of the London and South Western Railway. Unmanned halts were introduced to accommodate them and one was opened at Meyrick Park for a service between Bournemouth West and Christchurch; but as the line was extended it called at New Milton, Hinton Admiral and Ringwood. The halt was at the Wimborne Road end of Meyrick Park, not far from the entrance gates, and was intended for those living at Winton and for golfers 'to get an easier access to the links'. It ran seven times a day with room for about 40 passengers until it closed in 1917 as a wartime economy measure, never to re-open

Airfields

At the 1910 Bournemouth Centenary Celebrations, Britain's first International Aviation Meeting was held at Hengistbury Head. It is remembered today as marking the country's first fatal flying accident. On July 12 the tail of the Wright-Short biplane being flown by the Hon. C.S. Rolls snapped as he came in to land. His plane broke up in mid air, crashed, and Rolls was killed. *'It all seemed so very slow motion and there was hardly a sound'*, said an eye witness. A memorial plaque exists near the spot where he crashed in a corner of St Peter's School's fields (1978).

Baggage Transport

In the 1920s, visitors to the town could leave their luggage with an 'outside porter'. Each porter had a large hand-truck on which bags were loaded and he pushed to the appropriate destination. The porters wore a white metal arm band showing that they were licensed by the Council. Schoolboys would augment their pocket money by waiting at the station until all licensed porters were out on jobs, and then approach anyone carrying a bag with the greeting, 'Carry your bag, sir?'

The Hon. C.S. Rolls in his aircraft before his fatal accident at Southbourne in 1910, and a copy of the Souvenir card issued prior to the flight.

First Flight

The first Bournemouth flight to London was made in a Handley Page aircraft still bearing its Royal Flying Corps number. It was piloted by Lt. Col. William Sholto-Douglas who later played a major role in Fighter Command in the Battle of Britain in the Second World War.

A few months earlier, in May 1910, flying displays were given over Wallisdown, and a small aerodrome opened at Talbot Village in 1915, reputed to be 'one of the finest private ones in England'. Five aeroplanes could be housed in the hangar and members of the public were taken for flights at a charge of £3, a considerable sum. But these were available only when cadet pilots for the Royal Flying Corps were not being trained. The flying field transferred to Redhill within a few years.

Amy Johnson, the famous aviator, would land nearby, possibly where the University stands.

The Bournemouth Aviation Company opened the Talbot Village Aerodrome shortly after the outbreak of the First World War. Within months Ensbury Farm had been bought for Royal Flying Corps training. In 1918, it became RAF Winton, a station for the newly formed Royal Air Force, but within a year it shifted to Beaulieu and civilians took control once again. Sir Alan Cobham's Flying Circus later made use of it. Just before the end of the First World War there were two fatal air crashes on Redhill Common. After the War, the aerodrome was used for commercial flights until 1927.

The same area was used for horse racing (National Hunt rules) but it lasted for only a year between 1925-6 and its use as an aerodrome continued for another year. Greyhound racing was popular there for a while, but developers around Victoria Park bought the land for housing and soon Western Avenue and Leybourne Avenue were established.

Kinson Parish Council indicated it would not object to its change of use to a Race Course, in the hope that it would relieve the unemployment in the area; and the Inspector of Courses for the National Hunt Committee said 'the site is highly suitable'. There were the usual interminable delays. Mr. Bernard Mortimer was quoted in *The People* as saying: '*The fairest town in the South is where until a few years ago they would not light the streets on a Sunday, and on that day insisted on keeping the electric trains*

Schneider Trophy Air Race

This famous race for seaplanes was held locally in 1919 over a triangular course: Bournemouth – Swanage – Hengistbury Head, a distance of 18 nautical miles. The race was over ten laps of the course. Thick fog delayed the planes from taking off at the scheduled time, but when it lifted at 5 p.m. it was decided to start the race. The French entry was not ready as a six o'clock start had been expected, but the race went on. Eventually, only the Italian entry, Signor Janello's plane, completed the course. Then it was found that he had finished in an impossibly short time. Investigation showed that someone had placed a spare marker buoy in Studland Bay and Janello had turned here instead of continuing to Swanage.

As he was the only entrant to finish the course, he was awarded the Trophy, only for it to be withdrawn later by the International Aviation Authority. Italy had a consolation; it was given the right to hold the next Schneider Trophy Race.

The first race, in 1913, was won by France at an average speed of 45mph. Britain won the Trophy outright in 1931 after three successive victories. The speed attained on this occasion was 379 m.p.h..

in their sheds just to annoy visitors and residents. What a collection of the pious and pompous. So long as they could inconvenience the voters who put them there, they loved it. So you can guess the opposition there was to a race course in this holy of holies. A race course here, my dear sir, do you know where you are? This is not Southend-on-Sea but Bournemouth, yes, yes, my dear sir, Bournemouth, they said as they puffed out their cheeks.'

12,000 people attended the first meeting, because the press after an advance visit had eulogised about the course, and the *Evening Standard* called it 'the Ascot of the South coast', with one stand holding 3,000 and another 1,400. But the bookmakers thought it was more like a tea party than a race meeting. There were 22 meetings before the course closed and gave itself over to aircraft racing.

A disappointing 6,000 attended the first meeting of aircraft racing, but that it should take place on a Sunday was heavily criticised by some local clergy. A Mr. Reed shot at one of the aircraft and was later charged with attempted murder. The trial must have been amusing. Only 70 of the 218 pellets hit the plane, and as justification for pulling the trigger the accused said, *'Low flying affects my mother's nerves, disturbs my cattle, and some planes fly so low they take the heads off my red hot pokers.'* Two fatal crashes sealed the future of the races and the Royal Aero Club cancelled further meetings.

Greyhound Racing was tried out in January 1928, and about 2,000 attended. The usual letters of protest were received, but the Bournemouth Council decided they could do nothing as the track was, in those days, outside the civic boundaries. But the National Hunt Stewards banned greyhound racing if ever horse racing was to return.

Both the Racecourse and the Greyhound Companies by 1928 had to go into voluntary liquidation: insufficient profit was made; Poole Council threatened legal action to recover rates due; and nearby land was increasing in value because of housing estate building. Leybourne Avenue was the first development on the race course track.

Bournemouth is renowned for its International Airport at Hurn which is able to accommodate the largest civil and military aircraft, including Concorde and Boeing 747s. When other airports are unable to operate because of bad weather, Bournemouth can usually accept the diversions.

Hurn began life as an RAF station in 1941, when land was cleared and levelled to create three runways. Later it was used for pre D-Day glider training, paratroop training, for landing agents in Occupied France and dropping supplies to the Resistance. From September 1944 it was the principal terminal for BOAC. In 1966 the Civil Air Authority caused scheduled air services to end there; Dorset County and Bournemouth jointly bought the airport in 1969. It housed assembly shops for the Viscount and Valiant aircraft and gave employment to many Bournemouth people until 1984. In the 1990s, the airport was controversially sold to a private company for £4 million who made it more attractive. It has now returned to municipal ownership, but of Manchester City Council.

Today it is a small regional airport, but with both Thomson and Ryanair now flying scheduled flights to Europe and Ireland it is enjoying a welcome renaissance.

Richmond Terrace, Richmond Hill, about 1871. The Royal Norfolk Hotel has developed out of two of these villas.

Road Names

The Cooper Dean Estate: named from villages within a 10 mile radius of Bishop's Waltham and Meonstoke from where the family originated. Stokewood was the name of the family's house there. Bethia (after Edith Bethia Cooper-Dean d.1921); Cheriton, Colemore, Corhampton, Denmead, Droxford, Durrington, Exton, Hambledon, Hursley, Meon, Ovington, Petersfield, Ropley, Southwick, Swanmore, Waltham, Wharnford.

The Malmesbury Estate: Lord Malmesbury's seat was at Hurn (Heron) Court, Holdenhurst; Avon, Fitzharris, Heron Court, Orcheson.

The Shelley (Boscombe Manor) Estate: Florence (the poet's birthplace); Woolstonecraft (his mother); Hawkswood (married John Shelley); Michelgrove (m. into family); Watkin (friend); Crabton Close; Shelley Road.

The Boscombe Spa Estate was laid out by Sir Henry Drummond Wolff and some roads were named after his friends and his associations: Owls (after an occasional publication: 1864-70); Roumelia (Membership of Eastern Roumelia Commission 1878-80); Ashley, Churchill, Drummond, Randolph.

The Talbot Sisters had Scottish relations so: Talbot, Melville, Leven.

Early villas built in the town gave their names to roads: Albert, Firs, Parsonage, Knole, Verulam, Yelverton.

Then there are the obvious connections with **royalty**: Albert, Princess, Victoria. / King's, King Edward, Alexandra. / Coronation, King George, Queen Mary. / Harewood and Lascelles (Wedding of the Princess Royal to Earl of Harewood).

Prime Ministers: Gladstone, Palmerston, Rosebery, Salisbury.

Local MPs: Balfour (not the Prime Minister), Brassey (his defeated opponent by 3 votes), Haviland (Burke), Winston (when he was a member of Asquith's government), Randolph (Churchill's father).

Other MPs: Marquis of Lansdowne, Sir Stafford Northcote, a Chancellor of the Exchequer who became Lord Iddesleigh, Sir William Harcourt, Mr Speaker Lowther.

Liberal politicians: Roseberry, Harcourt, Granville, Morley.

Local Commissioners, Mayors and Councillors, etc.: Abbott, Barnes, Beechey, Bishop, Collingbourne, Frost, Holloway, Hosker, Luckham, McWilliam, Moore, Rebbeck, Russell-Cotes, Whitelegg. Bloomfield was Vicar of Moordown St John's; Ashling was Town Clerk from 1911-39; Hadow (Education Report); Benion (John Benion Jones, an early chief clerk in the local Education Department); Ibbett (Secretary to the Education Committee for 30 years).

The Duke of Argyll opened Boscombe Pier; Sir George Truscott, Lord Mayor of London, opened Bournemouth Pier; Cassell after Sir Edward Cassell; Zetland after 2nd Earl of Zetland.

Holders of the V. C. born locally: Noble, Riggs, Seagrim.

War leaders: Cardigan, Cromwell, Cunningham, Gort, Marlborough, Montgomery, Mountbatten, Roosevelt, Tedder, Wavell, Wellington. Pilot Hight (a NZ RAF Pilot Officer shot down and killed at Leven Avenue/Walsford Road, Talbot Woods. Plaque in St. Peter's Church).

Battles: Bengal, Crimea, Delhi, Jameson, Trafalgar.

Religious Figures: Calvin, Cranmer, Luther, Wycliffe.

Writers: Byron, Browning, Chaucer, Stevenson, Shakespeare, Shelley.

Above The horse trough and drinking fountain at the Lansdowne was gratefully used after the long, uphill trek from the centre of Bournemouth.

Below The Bournemouth Brewery with its Mineral Water Factory in Holdenhurst Road: since demolished.

Road Name Changes

The road given first is the name today.

Alton Rd was Park Rd
Ashley Rd was Cleveland Rd
Boscombe Arcade was Grand Continental Arcade
Boscombe Cres was Carnarvon Cres
Bourne Av was Bourne Valley Rd/ Sanatorium Rd
Capston Rd was Durnford Rd
Castle Lane was Strouden Av
Cemetery Junction was Rush Corner
Central Pleasure Gdns was Decoy Pond Meadow
Coombe Av was Quomp, Coombe Corner
Criterion Arcade was Post Office Av/ Town Hall Av
East Howe Lane was Headless Cross Lane
Firs Glen Rd was Church Glen Rd
Green Rd/Portland Rd was Hicks Common
Grove Rd was Boscombe Rd
Hinton Rd was Church Rd
Horseshoe Common was Wyndham's Acre
Joseph's Steps was Little Durley Chine
The Lansdowne was Six Cross Rd
Livingston Rd was Stanley Rd

Rush Corner
Rush Corner was an attractive part of Bournemouth famous for the rushes which grew profusely in the area. When the Council in 1903 decided to run a branch tramline from Wimborne Road to Winton, the name was changed to Cemetery Junction.

On the Ball

The 1877 edition of *Sydenham's Guide* reports: *'The observer can post himself up to the time of day by noting the electric ball at Messrs. Wyatt & Sons, Southbourne Terrace, which, in direct communication by wire with Greenwich Observatory, falls daily, Sunday excepted, at ten o'clock in the morning.*

Richmond Hill

Why should a main road to the east and north of the town be laid out up such a steep hill? It would be so much more convenient to use the flatter route closer to the Town Hall. It was to make it difficult for smugglers to haul their barrels of brandy up such a steep hill.

Queen's Park Drive

Underneath Queen's Park Drive is a pipe containing the stream which drained the heathland on which the Golf Course now stands. It was constructed in 1906, and a horse riding track was provided over it 'for the enjoyment of residents and visitors alike'. Additionally, this pipe takes drainage water from Talbot Woods and Winton and is 6 feet in diameter.

Meyrick Park was Marbarrow Valley
Muscliffe Farm was Muccleshell Farm
New Road Bridge was Ensbury Bridge
Pine Walk was Invalids' Walk
Pleasure Gardens was Bournemouth Park
Queen's Park Ave was Great Dean Bottom
Redhill Drive was Nurse Hill
Riverside Av was Longmoor Lane
Robert Louis Stevenson Av was Centre Rd /Middle Rd
Seamoor Rd was Crescent Rd
Shelbourne Rd was Fitzharris Rd
Slades Farm was Talbot Farm
Southbourne was The Guns
St Paul's Rd was Heath Poult Rd
St Peter's Rd was Gervis Rd
St Swithun's Rd was Railway Rd
Stafford Rd was Dispensary Rd
Talbot Av was Talbot Village Rd
Terrace Mount was Prospect Mount
Tregonwell Rd was Victoria Rd
Warren Edge Rd was Queen's Rd
West Westover Rd was Westover Plantations
Woodbury Av was Shiphouse Lane
Zig Zag Steps was Steps Chine

EIGHT

A Little Learning

Education and Schools

Bournemouth's Victorian Commissioners had no legal responsibility to provide education for the town's children until the passing of the 1870 Education Act. Private schools had already been set up, of course, called Dames' Schools, the first probably in Throop in 1825, and, in 1834, a Church of England school in Kinson. The first in the town centre was near where Debenham's is today. St Peter's School opened next door to St Peter's Church in 1850, remaining a school until its demolition in 1937 (where Bliss and Goadsby and Harding are now). Interestingly, the school was partly funded by the sale of a set of four lithographs, entitled 'Views of Bournemouth, Hants' by Harriet Daniell, who is buried in St Peter's churchyard. St. John's in Moordown followed in 1854, St. James at Pokesdown in 1856, and St. Paul's in 1866. St. Andrew's began in 1878, St. Clement's in 1888 and St. Ambrose's in 1892. The Free Churches also set up British Schools: at Winton in 1877, Westbourne in 1880 and Malmesbury Park Free in 1901. The first Roman Catholic Schools were St. Walburga's in Yelverton Road in 1877 and the Holy Cross, Boscombe, in 1889.

When the Education Act of 1870 decreed that School Boards should be set up to provide schools for the 5-13 year olds, there was initially no necessity for one in Bournemouth because the need was being met by various voluntary organisations. The town's population was naturally grateful because no education charges on the rates would have to be levied

Teaching in the 1920s

'I was appointed to Winton and Moordown Infants in 1927, straight out of training college. My class was of 60 five-year-olds in a classroom designed for 45 children.

There were no display boards, so that any good work done by the children had to be hung on string draped along the walls, for nothing was allowed to be stuck on the walls themselves.

The staff room was plain, with no facilities even to boil a kettle, so cups of tea or coffee were impossible. The staff room was also the base of a part-time teacher who gave individual teaching to children with special problems of learning.'

School Teachers' Salaries

With reference to the decision of the Education Committee that *'If the head teacher of any school neglects to send in a salaries return in time to be dealt with by the Committee, the salaries for that school be not paid until the month following'*. Councillor Mackenzie suggested it was not right to punish the teachers for the neglect of their head teachers. Alderman Mate said that the Committee was bound to take some steps to get the head teachers to do their duty in this respect.

Councillor Mackenzie: *'If we may take this as being only a brutal threat, I don't mind, but if carried out it would be most unjust'*.

Alderman Mate: *'No, you must not assume that'*.

Councillor Mackenzie: (jocularly) *'I hope Alderman Mate will take notice that it is 'most unjust' and 'brutal'.'*

Bournemouth Visitors' Directory, 5 June, 1909.

Pokesdown Mechanics Institute

This was formed in 1868 for older boys. It met at St. James' School for four years until its own premises were opened in Cromwell Road. There was a lecture room, a reading room and a club room for games.

The local temperance society held its meetings at the premises and a map of 1903 shows it as the Temperance Hall. The building is still in use.

The local Primitive Methodists used the building until they occupied their own in Hannington Road in 1897.

**Extracts from Council Minutes
17 September 1945**

An appeal to be made to the Ministry of Food to grant to grave diggers the same allowance of cheese as is granted to agricultural workmen.

The School Attendance Sub-committee name the parents to be prosecuted for not seeing their children attended school.

The parents of a boy who had perfect attendance for 3 years (1266 sessions) and was never late was sent the Committee's congratulations on this very creditable achievement.

Education Committee

Before 1974, meetings of the Committee were very formal. A member would indicate that he wished to speak. Nothing unusual about that, but when called by the Chairman, he or she would have to stand. Interjections were just not done. And officers were never permitted to voice their opinions. I well remember the Music Adviser saying, 'I would advise you to . . .' and Alderman Bill Wareham jumping to his feet and saying, 'On a point of order . . . How dare this officer suggest to this committee what it should or should not do. He presents the facts, we make the decisions'. That was putting it mildly. I've never forgotten his interjection after over thirty years.

as the church was providing all that was necessary, except in Kinson and Talbot Village, which were in Dorset not Hampshire.

The reliance on church schools was to last until the 1902 Education Act stipulated that teachers' salaries in church schools had to be paid from the rates and government grants. High church and low church in the Anglican communion couldn't agree about this; so how could Free Churches, Roman Catholics and Anglicans be expected to show a united front? Respectable members of Richmond Hill Congregational Church, led by a future Mayor, Mr. Bright, refused to pay their rates over the issue, and they were joined by many others. It all seemed to calm down until it was revealed that most of these voluntary schools left much to be desired: overcrowding, lack of proper sanitation, inadequate heating.

In 1886 there were thirty-two private schools in the town, and the *Bournemouth Guide* for 1912 had ten pages of advertisements for them, mostly for girls' schools, '*the town's mild climate being considered desirable for them*'. Boys were not so fortunate. They '*were sent away to boarding schools, where healthy hardships would fulfil their education*'.

The Education Committee grudgingly took up an offer by Hampshire County Council of £2,300 and matched it with a similar amount to open the first Secondary and Technical School in the town in January 1901 with 54 boys. A preparatory department opened a year later. The school was in Portchester Road. Two years later, 'Technical' was dropped from the title and it became Bournemouth School. The woodwork room was made available for limited periods to boys from the elementary schools. Later, Lowther Road Hospital was taken over as accommodation for the junior forms whilst the upper forms remained at Portchester Road.

The Council offered scholarships for suitable girls to attend a private school, but often there were insufficient places for them. However, the Council happily opened the Bournemouth West School of Art and Science on Poole Hill, and the East Bournemouth School of Art, Science and Technical Instruction in Drummond Road, Pokesdown, now a clinic. Difficulties were experienced in staffing them both.

Alma Road School was built in 1906 and at the opening celebratory tea the chairman, Alderman Mate, was forced to answer criticism that '*the buildings are too large and too expensive,*' He argued that the population was increasing rapidly, and was proved right. It started with 658 on the roll and within four years there were over a thousand pupils.

In the summer of 1905 a Celebration of Education was held in Meyrick Park to mark the changes that had been made in the education provision in the town since the 1902 Act. Unofficially, it was also a celebration for the bringing together of the ecclesiastical warring factions over church schools and state schools. The *Bournemouth Guardian* wrote, '*The event formed one of the most charming spectacles witnessed in Bournemouth*'. Seven thousand children attended in the Park, the senior children marching there, the infants brought in 20 tramcars. The two local military bands and the Postmen's Band, the Winton Prize Band and part of the Municipal Orchestra in turn accompanied flag-carrying processions of children. It was estimated that a crowd of 18,000 gathered in the Park to welcome them and watch the sports competitions, in which 1,800 young male athletes took part.

But parents of girls were now lobbying and petitioning the Committee to hasten the provision of a girls' secondary school. It took a further twelve years, and the immense social changes brought about by the First World War, before Bournemouth School for Girls formally opened on January 30 1918. 'BSG', as it is usually known, is now at Castle Gate Close, Castle Lane, down the hill from Bournemouth School – which should never be called Bournemouth School for Boys or 'BS'.

After the Education Act of 1944, the word 'elementary' was not used for schools any more: they were to be 'Secondary' or 'Primary', 'Junior' or 'Infants'. Bournemouth's Secondaries at that time were Alma Road Girls, Boscombe Senior, East Howe Boys, East Howe Girls, Portchester Road Boys, and Beaufort Senior. The following secondary schools opened within a decade: Oakmead Girls, Oakmead Boys, Avonbourne Girls, Glenmoor Girls, and Summerbee.

The school leaving age was raised to fifteen in 1957, so additional accommodation was quickly required at minimal expense, and prefabricated class rooms were erected where necessary (ROSLA blocks). Only very recently have they been replaced.

The 2001 Census showed that Bournemouth had the 347th smallest number of under sixteens out of 360 authorities in the country. There were 21 schools in 1903, of which 13 were run by the Church of England, and there were 7,599 children of school age. In 2003, there are eleven secondary schools and 22 primary schools to cater for 19,115 children.

The Borough has two selective grammar schools, one for boys, the other for girls, and 16% of local children entering secondary level attend them. Those not in that 16% attend one of the six other secondary schools, known as 'bi-lateral' schools because each offers education to GCSE, which is possible because such a low percentage of pupils are admitted to the grammar schools. Bournemouth was thus one of the first and few authorities in the country to provide '0' Levels in all secondary schools back in the mid-1950s. This was known as the Smedley Plan, after the then Director of Education. Pupils of proved ability are able to transfer to the sixth form of the grammar schools or to the Municipal College to study for 'A' Levels.

However, there is one Roman Catholic Comprehensive (St. Peter's) which, because it has its own sixth form, influences intakes slightly, on denominational and educational grounds. From September 2004, Summerbee became the first Church of England Secondary School in Bournemouth, calling itself the Bishop of Winchester Comprehensive School, although children in the north of Bournemouth are in the Bishop of Salisbury's Diocese.

Today, all are 'Secondary Schools'. Oakmead used to be a Boys' School and a Girls' School; King's High School was formerly Kingsleigh, and before that East Howe Boys' and East Howe Girls'.

Clingham Bequest
The Clingham Charity took over the management of the farm at Iford when Mr. Harvey died in 1907, but allowed his daughter to live there until they decided to demolish the farm in the 1930s. They offered Miss Harvey the chance to take anything from it to her new home. She chose the front and back door steps so she could continue to cross the same thresholds she had always done. Grants are made by the Clingham Trust to local school children.

St. Michael's School
This was for the teaching of *'children and adults, or children only, of the labouring, manufacturing and other poorer classes in the said district of St Michael'*.
  A church committee had the sole rights to select the books to be used in the school.

St Mark's School Log
15th September, 1898. A violent thunder storm. Only one child came to school (out of 92).
1887. A bad outbreak of Scarletina kept the school closed from October to January!
1881. Girl sent home for arrears of school fees of 1/1 (5 p).
May, 1919. Loss of the school crops because of 48 days without rain.

Difficulties

Wet and windy weather affected attendance 75 years ago. There was no public transport and roads were mostly untarmacked. Children had to walk to and from school not only in the mornings and afternoons but also at lunch times. That was why the 'dinner' break was two hours from 12-2.

Regulations and Suggestions for Managers for Elementary Schools, 1903,

'All communications with the Education Committee must be written on foolscap paper, and on one side only, with a margin on the left hand side of each page.'

In 1908, the Committee decided not to employ married women teachers in permanent posts. Women teachers had to resign when they married.

Alma Road School was destroyed by a land mine in November 1940, and Westbourne School was so severely damaged as to be unuseable until 1946.

Secondary

Avonbourne (Girls)
Bicknell (Special)
Bournemouth School (Boys' Grammar)
Bournemouth School for Girls (Grammar)
Glenmoor (Girls)
Kings High (mixed)
Linwood (Special)
Oakmead College of Technology (mixed)
Portchester (Boys)
St. Peter's (R.C. mixed comprehensive)
Bishop of Winchester Comprehensive (C of E, mixed)
Winton (Boys)

Private

Talbot Heath (Secondary Girls) Rothesay Rd,
Talbot House, Firs Glen Rd,
Wentworth College (Secondary Girls) College Rd
Bournemouth Jewish Day
Dewlish House, Howard Road
The Park School, Queen's Park
St Martin's, Stokewood Road
St Thomas Garnet's (RC)

Primary

Bethany (C of E)
Christ the King (RC)
Corpus Christi (RC)
Elmrise
Epiphany (C of E)
Heathlands
Hill View
Kings Park
Kingsleigh
Kinson
Malmesbury Park
Moordown St John's (C of E)
Muscliff
Pokesdown Community
Queen's Park (Summerbee)
St Clement's & St John's (C of E)
St James (C of E)
St Katharine's (C of E)
St Luke's (C of E)
St Mark's (C of E)
St Michael's (C of E)
St Walburga's (RC)
Stourfield
Townsend
Winton

The entrance to Poole House, Bournemouth University.

The Municipal College and University

Complete with a central library and a clock tower, the Municipal College opened in 1910. The tower was nicknamed 'Mate's Folly' because the clock face had no numbers, just a simple line for each instead, and Mate was the then Chairman of the Education Committee. The Department of Commerce and Language moved to Knyveton Road in 1947 into a converted hotel which had been occupied during the War by a domestic college from London. When Bournemouth School for Girls went from Gervis Road to new premises at Castle Lane in 1960, the College expanded into their old buildings.

It then became the Dorset Institute of Further Education. In 1991 it became a Polytechnic, and a year later Bournemouth University with, in 2005, a total of 15,000 students. Its main teaching buildings are housed at the Talbot Campus, which geographically is in Poole, across the road from Talbot Village. The other buildings are at The Lansdowne.

Foreign Language Schools

Education has overtaken Tourism as the major industry in Bournemouth. In addition to over 12,000 University students, Foreign Language schools bring in an estimated £200 million a year to the local economy, nearly three times more than visitors who stay in hotels.

There are 20 accredited foreign language schools in the town and over 90 per cent of their students stay in local homes for an average of ten weeks.

Bournemouth now takes 10% of the United Kingdom's market in teaching English as a foreign language to those from abroad.

Right The Baths and Sydenham's Library as it was in 1865. It was pulled down in 1935 to make way for the Pier Approach Baths, which, in turn, became The Waterfront Centre in 1999 (*below right*) containing the reviled IMAX.

Libraries

John Sydenham, the Poole bookseller, opened a Library and Reading Room attached to the Belle Vue Boarding House in 1840. It stood on the site now occupied by the Pavilion, and was advertised to have '*a plentiful supply of books, magazines, and newspapers (which) proffered information as to the course of the busy world and presented sources of intellectual amusement and recreation*'. Unlike modern libraries, it also sold soda water, lemonade, tea, coffee, sheet music and pianos.

The early days of the town were largely democratic. Votes were taken by the residents on nearly everything of importance, but an 1885 vote to provide public libraries was defeated 914 to 749. A second vote, after the passing of the Public Libraries Act in 1893, produced a majority of 2,062 votes for to 704 against, thanks to the campaigning of C.J. Whitting who went on to serve on the Library committee for 32 years.

The Town Council was now able to adopt the Public Libraries Act, and in the first year the equivalent of a penny rate (£1,100) was allocated for the Book Sub Committee to buy 4,500 volumes. And residents and 'gentlemen living in London and elsewhere' donated additional books to the purchase. These books were stored at the Library Offices in Yelverton

Road because the library itself had not yet been built! From the beginning, it was decided that branches should be established in places where voters lived, not just in the centre of the town.

The first Bournemouth library opened at Cumnor Terrace, Old Christchurch Road, with a reading room in Boscombe, on 1 January, 1895. Other libraries were to follow at Springbourne and Westbourne. Thanks to Andrew Carnegie, the Scottish philanthropist, the town received £10,000 in 1903 for the building of libraries. The first to be built with his money was the one at Winton on land given by the Earl of Leven and Melville. It has a plaque outside recording their generosity. The site for Springbourne's was given by the Council and the original library at Boscombe was paid for by public subscription.

Charminster Library has an abundance of space which the public never sees. Hidden from view is a most gloriously designed wooden screen about 15 feet high, 5 feet short of the ceiling; no one appears to know why this was built. Strouden Library, previously a small, prefabricated building, was replaced by a modern building as part of 'the deal' with the giant Castlepoint development on Castle Lane.

The Central Library, which for years was at the Lansdowne under the clock tower, was cramped and old fashioned. It was difficult to find sitting spaces at the tables in the Reference Section because they were usually occupied by students from the College which shared the building. The Lending Library was made to look larger by mirrors fixed to the recesses of each window so each mirror would reflect the other. They made no difference except in the mind of the then Chairman of the Libraries sub-Committee who had given orders for this to be done. A replacement Central library was built by Private Finance Initiative ('P.F.I.') at the Triangle and opened in 2002. On long-term display there is the enormous oil on canvas *Adoration of the Sea* by Nicholas Charles Williams, measuring 625 cm by 305 cm. A window had to be removed to get it in. This Library has an extensive Local History section and the Music Library is well known all over the country.

True Fiction
Except in the case of the works of about half-a-dozen modern standard novelists, fiction is not purchased until public opinion has decided in its favour. The plan has worked well for a number of years, and the committee sees no necessity to deviate from it. It is considered that it is no part of the functions of a Public Library Committee to provide novels as fast as they are poured out of the press at the present.
(early 1900s)

Thanks to Donors
The Library Sub-Committee at its meeting 14 April 1930 thanked donors of books. The Minutes list that *Successful Poultry Farming*, *The History of Nigeria* and Virginia Woolf's *A Room of One's Own* were purchased in addition to 1,771 volumes of adult and juvenile fiction.

The new Central Library at The Triangle, opened in 2002.

Merton Russell-Cotes (1835-1921) became the only Mayor of Bournemouth (1893-4) who was not a Councillor. He was made a Freeman of the Borough in 1908 and was knighted a year later.

Right The Russell-Cotes Museum, photographed in 1907 when it was still called East Cliff Hall and was Merton and Annie Russell-Cotes's private house.

Below The interior of East Cliff Hall.

Russell-Cotes Museum and Art Gallery

In 1880 Merton and Annie Russell-Cotes acquired The Royal Bath Hotel, going on to fill it with the vast collection of objects and paintings amassed by them in their world-wide travels. To see the collection was one of the attractions of staying at the hotel, and it was very much a reflection of Russell-Cotes's own taste. As well as Japanese art, 18th and 19th century ceramics (including a fine group of Wedgwood jasperware), 18th and 19th century silver and plate, Russell-Cotes collected a large number of Victorian and Edwardian paintings, and memorabilia and theatrical relics relating to Sir Henry Irving, with whom he was friends.

Later, as Sir Merton and Mayor of Bournemouth, Russell-Cotes built the present Russell-Cotes Museum as a birthday present for his wife in 1894. Originally called East Cliff Hall, and their private house, it was very much in the style of an Italianate seaside villa with covered verandahs and a mosaic ornamented hall. On its completion, Sir Merton announced that he would give a large part of his art collection and Annie would give the house and most of its contents to the town, provided they could live there during their lifetimes.

New galleries were added to the house after Sir Merton's death, and it was opened as The Russell-Cotes Museum and Art Gallery by Princess Beatrice, Queen Victoria's youngest daughter, in 1919, when the collection consisted of 250 paintings and 60 sculptures. A fourth gallery was opened in 1926 and a modern extension in 1989. Curiously, it was in the Curator's job description that he and his family should live in a flat provided in the base of the building, yet many of the exhibits were in storage and could not be displayed for lack of space (Edward Long's painting *Flight into Egypt* is 16 feet long). Residence here is no longer a condition. In 1941, the curator laid clay over part of the terrace and flooded it so it could be used for ice skating in winter. Cold winters are now rare, and the original gardens have been restored.

One of the more idiosyncratic items in the collection was the **Geological Terrace**, erected in the 1950s and consisiting of 194 different varieties of rock. Each of them was freely given by the quarry owners and (with some exceptions such as County Councils) freely transported to the site. There were a few gaps to accommodate additional specimens which might be filled when quarry workings began on pre-Cambrian formations. Their order was selected by an expert from the Natural History Museum. The chisel marks on the stones were not mason's marks but were done on site as an identity check. The Terrace was dismantled in the mid-1990s and stored at Southcote Road Depot, then transferred to one of the Portsmouth forts and then returned to be stored once again in Bournemouth. It was supposed to return to the Museum walls, but in 2005 it was re-erected outside Bournemouth University at the Talbot Campus. It was always a popular attraction, especially with children.

The great storm of 1987 damaged the exterior of the building and it was obvious that a vast sum of money would have to be spent if it were to continue in its Edwardian splendour. A £2m Heritage Lottery Grant and a Council contribution were obtained. Research was undertaken to redecorate the interior so that it would be as it was when Merton Russell-Cotes was alive; and the garden restored to its design of 1921. It was reopened in 2001 by the Duke of Gloucester.

Above One of the small, metal sculptures attached to the railings on the south path behind the Museum leading to the sea front.

Below The Geological Terrace formerly at the south of the Museum. In 2005 it was re-erected at the Talbot Campus, Bournemouth University.

The Mystery of the Russell-Cotes War Memorial

The Russell-Cotes War Memorial was unveiled by the Countess of Malmesbury on 27 July 1926. It was in the garden on the south side of the new Art Gallery opened on that same day. The Memorial faced the sea looking towards the pier, and was about 30 feet high. It was of a soldier, a sailor and an airman, with a woman holding a laurel wreath in each of her outstretched hands standing behind them. All figures were at least life-size and were sculpted in Portland stone by George Maile. They stood on what was to turn out to be a very robust plinth.

The Memorial had been given to the town at the request of Sir Merton Russell-Cotes by his two adult children. A brass plaque on the plinth reads:

'1914-1918 To the unknown dead of All Services who died in The Cause of Liberty this Monument is erected in grateful memory by Herbert Russell-Cotes and Ella Stebbing.'

Although both were present at the ceremony, mysteriously neither was invited to open the Art Gallery nor to unveil the War Memorial.

It had been recommended by the Borough Engineer that the Memorial should stand in the Musuem garden, and the sub-Committee, which had power to act over this, agreed with his suggestion. By March 1925, a

The War Memorial at the south side of the Russell-Cotes Museum. It mysteriously disappeared although the figures were all life size.

Portrait Medallions

Portrait medallions of Milton, Burns, Shakespeare, Walter Scott, Bacon, Beethoven, Handel and Chaucer are set into the exterior south wall of the Museum. They were placed there in 1926 but why and by whom is not known.

month later, the sub-Committee had changed its mind and decided on a different site: the north side of the Art Gallery in Russell-Cotes Road.

Within two months the Memorial had been erected on the south side of the Gallery.

Minutes do not record why there was a change of mind, nor why the Borough Engineer took no notice of his committee's decision. The sub-Committee inspected the sculpture in its place and ordered that the hedge in front of it should be removed. Presumably this was to allow people walking down the south pathway to the Pier to be able to view the Memorial.

In 1941, damage to the rifle of the Sailor was reported. It had been blown off and the rumour was that it had fallen on a gardener. Three years later, the curator reported that the Memorial needed repair. Within a year the decision was made to remove the 20-year-old Memorial because it was in a dilapidated state. A new one was to be commissioned to stand on the original plinth.

Five years later, in 1950, 'consents' had been obtained to remove the Memorial, and a plan for a 'geological wall' was approved so that even the plinth could be removed. There was to be no replacement Memorial as had previously been agreed.

The plinth was carefully to be dug out in case it could be used elsewhere. It was discovered that it was '*unnecessarily and tremendously*' strong for the purpose of supporting four life-size figures, and concern was expressed that it might have been placed there as '*an anchor to the art galleries when it was feared that the proximity to the cliff might cause a settlement*'.

The next month the Borough Engineer was able to report there need be no danger, but the cost of the removal would increase by £200 to £600.

The plinth was apparently broken up and disposed of in a tip or used as rubble. But what happened to the four figures, sculpted by a relatively well-known sculptor? That is the second mystery. They were perhaps damaged by the winds blowing from the sea. But they were carved out of Portland stone and were only 25 years old. There are Portland stone buildings on Portland that are 300 years old and still in good condition. Perhaps they were broken up and suffered the same fate as the plinth. The workmen employed to destroy it would remember what World War the Memorial commemorated and would surely have spoken to someone about what they were being asked to do. Nobody seems to know.

Perhaps the sub-Committee members were right to change their minds and ask that it be put on the opposite side of the building out of the way of the sea winds. Would the Memorial still be there in all its glory if the Borough Engineer had taken notice of the instruction? Did the Members of the sub-Committee realise the damage that the winds would cause? Or had they left it too late for the unveiling that was to take place four months later?

The Rothesay Museum occupied for a time a former Bournemouth Transport building opposite the Pier Approach Bath. It housed a collection

of 350 typewriters. Memorabilia of the poet Shelley were at Shelley Park, but this Museum was closed in the 1980s when the honorary curator died. Its contents were distributed to more appropriate museums or put into storage, but one day may be reassembled at Shelley Manor, Boscombe.

The Pier Approach Baths, 1936-1998. The building in the background on the left was a bus station which was converted into the Rothesay Museum before being pulled down to make space for a car park.

The Bournemouth Natural Science Society's building, contents and grounds at 39 Old Christchurch Road is without doubt the town's best kept secret. It contains displays of stuffed birds, birds eggs, insects and butterflies. Horns of beasts adorn the walls. There are ancient Egyptian remains to see, and the collections of geological and botanical specimens are unique in the south of England. The lovely garden, with unusual plants and trees, is lovingly tended by members of the Society.

Prominently displayed in the entry lobby of the building is this notice:

Before the days of videos and colourful textbooks, it was only possible to study animals and plants by collecting specimens. This has been the foundation of natural history research and knowledge. It has been done at a cost to wildlife and such collecting is now both illegal and unethical.

The Bournemouth Natural Science Society supports and embraces measures to stop taking from the wild and no longer collects live specimens of plants or animals.

The displays around these rooms are the vestige of the earlier days when collecting was the norm. Whilst we may regret these animals being killed, we would not wish to compound the damage by disposing of the specimens. They still have a valuable role in instructing and providing wonder.

Lectures are frequently given on appropriate subjects in the Society's comfortable 100 seat theatre, which is also used for a fortnight in June/July for music and drama by The Bournemouth Music Competitions Festival. This Festival, which also includes dance, began in 1927 and attracts over 2000 entrants aged between 4 and 94.

NINE

Broadcasting & the Press

Radio

Bournemouth played its part in the birth of radio. Madeira House, west of the Pier, had an aerial in its garden erected by Guglielmo Marconi. In 1898, it received the first commercial wireless message from the Isle of Wight, and Marconi made more experiments from the Haven Hotel, Sandbanks. By 1922, Bournemouth had a School of Wireless in Lansdowne Road, and a year later loud speakers were erected in the Square, by the Arcades and at a few other places to listen to the first broadcasts. The local studios were in Holdenhurst Road and later in Bushey Road, Charminster; local programmes were broadcast for three hours daily on 382 metres. Members of Bournemouth Little Theatre Club were summoned to take part in the broadcast plays. In 1939, the BBC opened a studio in Westover Road, and for four years local bands and orchestras, mostly professional, were broadcast.

Bayley & Sons, Poole Hill, were licensed by the Postmaster General to provide live performances of orchestras from London through telephone headphones. It is said that on Sundays, 15 different church services could be heard, but this was probably an exaggerated report.

BBC Radio Solent began in 1970 and, in 1980, the local commercial radio station, 2CR, began with studios in Southcote Road. ITV and BBC both present early evening local news television transmissions, and Bournemouth seems to have its fair share of time in the programmes. Radio Solent has a small room in the Town Hall which is equipped with the necessary microphone for local people to broadcast live to avoid the journey to studios at Southampton. Wave 105 is also received locally and is used by many for the road reports which are broadcast at regular intervals. There is a Christian radio station, Hope FM, broadcasting from the YMCA in Westover Road, but few have heard it or know of its existence.

Local Radio

When tenders for the local broadcasting franchise were being examined, one of the applicants was asked at the interview, 'Why haven't you submitted a typical week's programme?'

This consortium replied, 'We don't wish any of the rival companies to be able to steal any of our ideas'. Needless to say, this applicant was not successful.

Newspapers

The Bournemouth Visitors' Directory (1858-75), *The Bournemouth Observer and Chronicle* (1875-1908), and *The Bournemouth Guardian* (1893-1928) were the town's early newspapers. *The Bournemouth Graphic* (1902-1935) published mostly photographs.

The Bournemouth Times (out of which evolved the *Advertiser)*, was a weekly newspaper with plenty of pictures. It had a popular item called 'Genevieve's Column' which listed those socialites who were present at

The original *Daily Echo* building, Richmond Hill.

various parties and dances. Many say the paper's circulation depended on those anxious to see who was at whose party or event.

The Enquirer was a privately owned, weekly give-away newspaper, crusading and lively, which lasted for a short time in the early 1970s. It failed to attract the required amount of advertising to keep it going and, much to the regret of many, it stopped publication.

The Daily Echo was founded in 1902 (circulation now 35,239; readership 100,758) and continues to keep everyone informed of the local political, arts and crime scenes etc. The pages devoted to the town's past are especially popular, and the paper includes various supplements throughout the week. A large number of readers buy it for the classified advertisements alone, and the Letters to the Editor section never fails to register series of opinions which mostly criticise the policies of the local councils. Brendan Carlin was the feared yet highly respected journalist who reported on Bournemouth's local government affairs, and he is still whispered about with reverence amongst some of the older local politicians.

The Advertiser (circulation 158,751, readership 226,674) is distributed free once a week and appears to have no difficulty in attracting advertising to keep it going.

The Bournemouth Journal is published in colour, bi-monthly and distributed free to every dwelling by Bournemouth Borough Council to provide a somewhat selective review of what the Council is up to.

High Society Arrives and Departs

The *Bournemouth Guardian* regularly listed polite society's comings and goings. Thus in November 1883: 'Amongst the latest arrivals are the Bishop of Ripon who intends staying through the winter months, and the Duke and Duchess of Norfolk who are staying at Stewart's Hotel; Lord and Lady Dalkeith; Viscountess Maidstone; the Dean of Gloucester; Lady and Miss Shakespeare; Lady Claverling; General and Mrs Younghusband; and Sir Edward and Miss Baines'.

Very much later, the weekly *Bournemouth Times* had a popular column written by Genevieve. Everyone knew it was Ken Baily, the well-known England cheer leader. He attended every public social occasion and listed the names of those who were there. There was no other gossip. His favourite expressions, used over and over again, were, 'Very much in evidence were . . .' and 'Bill Bloggs, the stalwart hockey player, with Miss Smith'. Conversation during the week amongst readers was, 'Saw your name in Genevieve's Column'. Only occasionally did people complain to the Editor that they weren't actually *with* Miss Smith.

Four views of The Square.

The first is from the early 1920s when there was a tall pole in the centre surrounded by grass. The second shows the tram/bus covered waiting rooms of the early 1930s. The third dates to 1943 just after the new traffic island had been completed, whilst the fourth shows the pedestrianised Square as it is today.

TEN

Buildings

Hotels

The hotels in the town have always been luxurious because it was the wealthy who went away, often for weeks at a time, taking with them their own servants. Many of the early villas were built for the rich to rent, who came not to be by the seaside but to benefit from the health-giving properties of the pines and to enjoy the warmer weather that the town boasted about.

It was not until the arrival of the railway in 1870 that small guest houses sprang up to cater for the less well off, who usually stayed for a week or a fortnight. Shops multiplied to cater for the day trippers who arrived in their thousands.

The (Royal) Bath Hotel was one of the earliest, opening in 1838. On Christmas Day 1876 it was bought by the Glasgow hotelier, Merton Russell-Cotes, who added two wings and used the hotel to display his collections. By 1891 it was being described as 'the showpiece of Bournemouth'. After staying there, Oscar Wilde wrote in the visitors' book: '*You have built and fitted up with the greatest beauty and elegance, a palace, and filled it with gems of art for the use and benefit of the public at hotel prices*'.

Benjamin Disraeli was another beneficiary of its comforts. Queen Victoria's physician suggested that he '*Try the very salubrious air of Bournemouth*'. He spent nearly three months at the hotel, even though he was Prime Minister at the time (1874-5).

According to Peter Pugh in his book about the hotel, Merton Russell-Cotes '*was clearly a snob and a name dropper*'. His wife, Annie, had '*a magnificent contralto voice*'.

Bright's Illustrated Guide to Bournemouth published in 1888 – which changes hands today for nearly £100 – has 22 pages of advertisements, five for hotels. The Royal Exeter Hotel still contains, amongst its many enlargements, the first house built in Bournemouth – Lewis Tregonwell's house of 1810. It was originally called Newlyn's Family Hotel, after its proprietor Henry Newlyn, who used his previous employment as manager of the Guard's Club in London to attract the fashionable and aristocratic, and went on to become twice mayor of Bournemouth. After being renamed again, as the even grander Royal and Imperial Exeter Park Hotel, it found favour with Her Imperial Majesty the Empress Elisabeth of Austria, who stayed there for ten days in 1888, bringing with her 30 servants and seven tons of luggage. None of them could speak English which on the first day led to some difficulties. The quick-thinking

Belle Vue Hotel
The Belle Vue was built at the same time as the Bath Hotel and both were opened in 1836. Sydenham's Library was added to it in 1840, and a few years later Assembly Rooms were added.

The hotel was situated immediately on the seaward side of the present Pavilion and was known as the Boarding House to distinguish it from its more opulent neighbour, the Bath Hotel. With its Assembly Rooms, the Boarding House became the centre of community and social life in Bournemouth and the premises were used extensively for meetings, concerts, entertainments, dances, and for religious services by those denominations who had no place of worship of their own.

The buildings were purchased by Bournemouth Corporation in 1906 in order to accelerate the building of a pavilion. In 1924, the Belle Vue Tap was demolished to make way for the Pavilion, but the Boarding House survived until the Pavilion opened in 1929. It was then reduced to rubble and its liquor licence transferred to the Pavilion.

Weston Hall Hotel Brochure, 1892
Mr Ratcliffe is aware that there are numerous 'Boarding Houses' in Bournemouth where visitors are received for a few shillings per day, but he wishes it to be understood that he does not cultivate the support of those who are satisfied with the fare and society obtainable at those Houses. He knows it impossible to please 'everybody' but assures Visitors that every effort is made by Mrs Ratcliffe and himself to promote the comfort and pleasure of the guests.

The Royal Bath Hotel in about 1880.

gardener then donned sandwich boards, on one side of which was written 'Seawater' and on the other side 'Milk' in German. The cow was housed in the stables opposite the hotel and the Empress's personal physician had to inspect its milk before it was delivered to her. Alas, the concern for her health did her little long-term good. Ten years later she was assassinated.

The Burlington in Owls Road is a deceptively early hotel for Bournemouth as it does not look 100 years old. In fact, it was built in 1893. Its exterior style is Italian Renaissance and, with its 200 rooms, it was the largest hotel in Bournemouth until it was converted into flats. In the lower ground floor there was a tiny theatre which was used in the 1950s by a professional repertory company.

The house that later became the Langtry Manor Hotel was built by Edward VII for his mistress, Lillie Langtry, and is reputed to be haunted. It is one of the smaller, luxurious hotels of Bournemouth.

The Carlton Hotel became a 5 star hotel in 1934 after the original buildings had been enlarged by connection to adjoining properties. The

Carlton Hotel
The Carlton Hotel on the East Cliff was used by the American Red Cross during the Second World War. In 1946, it became a transit station for British GI brides and their babies prior to sailing to America on the *Queen Mary*.

The Boscombe Chine Hotel.

press wrote, *'Inside the Carlton is luxury itself'*. The Hotel affords visitors *'who desire privacy, all the air and exercise they require without leaving the estate.'* The Boscombe Chine Hotel (where *'sanitary arrangements are perfect'*); Newlyn's Royal Exeter Park Hotel (*'patronised by the Royal Families of Europe and Nobility'*); the Imperial (*'the finest position on the East Cliff and the Imperial Omnibus meets all trains'*); and the Hotel Mont Dore (which can boast *'the most varied and perfect system of BATHS in the Kingdom, including Turkish, Sea Water, Pine and other Baths'*) are all listed in the Guide.

Slightly more humble were the three *'First-Class Boarding Establishments'* advertised by Joseph Dines. The Osborne in Exeter Road *'has passages heated with warm water which are kept at an even temperature of 60°*. The Dunedin in Priory Road, *'has lofty rooms connected with the Osborne'*, and Durlstone House on the South Cliff is with *'extensive views – the finest in Hampshire . . . and five minutes' walk to principal places of worship'*.

The Highcliff Hotel, used today by Prime Ministers when party conferences are held at the International Centre, has some Victorian coastguard cottages in the grounds; but they have been luxuriously restored. There is a small resort to the east of Bournemouth called Highcliffe. To avoid confusion, a coin was tossed to decide which would lose the 'e'. The Bournemouth Hotel lost.

Three other famous, large hotels no longer exist: the Grand in Fir Vale Road, the Imperial (The Round House) at the Lansdowne and the Linden Hall Hydro opposite Boscombe Gardens. The Hotel Metropole, now the Royal London House, at the Lansdowne offered *'a musical dinner every evening'*. It was destroyed by enemy aircraft on 23 May 1943, the same day that the Central Hotel was destroyed. The Priory Mansion on the East Cliff advertised that it was proud of its drainage. Miss Perman at St Clare, Exeter Road, advertised she is *'unvarying in her kindness and attention'*, whilst Augustus Young of the Continental on the Southcliff announced that he was late chef to the Earl of Tankerville!

In 1930, there were 2,599 hotels and guest houses in Bournemouth. In 2004, Bournemouth Tourism had 250 registered in its books and the Yellow Pages directory listed 83 guest houses, 233 hotels and 29 holiday flats with a Bournemouth address. Without the Bournemouth International Centre and the larger hotels offering smaller conference facilities, this number would be much depleted.

Churches

There appears to be an over-provision of churches in Bournemouth as few of the more traditional churches seem to have anywhere near a large congregation, except on special occasions. This observation is based on a private survey taken in 1999. In recent years, St. Paul's at Central Station, Holy Trinity, and St. Mary's, Holdenhurst Road, have all closed. St. Swithun's ceased to be an Anglican Church but has been successfully revitalised as one of the spreading evangelical community churches. In

2004, St. Andrew's Presbyterian Church in the Square was another casualty. Many of the Free Churches are experiencing small, elderly congregations and some ministers are undoubtedly anxious about the difficulties they are facing in attracting younger families.

Bournemouth's first Anglican church was a temporary building near the Decoy Pond, which was converted from a pair of semi-detached cottages and also served as a school. There was also a mud and thatch Congregational Chapel at Pokesdown. Sir George Gervis's plans for the new town always included the building of a proper Anglican church, and St Peter's was finally consecrated by the Bishop of Winchester in August 1845. Its first vicar was the dynamic Morden Bennett, who called it 'a very poor structure': a contemporary architectural journal was even blunter, describing it as 'unmitigated ugliness and hopeless inconvenience'. Morden Bennett gradually transformed its fortunes. The school opened in 1850 and extensions and alterations to the church by the architect George Edmund Street (who also designed the Royal Courts of Justice in London) turned it into a much more substantial building.

By 1869 the work was complete. Sadly, the cock on top of the spire, the symbol of St. Peter, majestically crowed for only two years before it was blown off its perch in a storm. It was replaced with a lighter cross which makes the height of the church 202 feet, exactly half the height of Salisbury Cathedral, . Within a year, both Morden Bennett and Street were dead.

The Wooden Pier and the East Beach in about 1875, showing the tower of St Peter's Church before the addition of its spire

The First St. Peter's
The first St Peter's, opened in 1843, was small: the stipend was apparently even smaller. No clergyman could be attracted to accept the living, so for two years the building remained unconsecrated, although it was licensed for services. Fortunately for Bournemouth, the wealthy Revd. Alexander Morden Bennett had married as his second wife a lady whose family lived in Christchurch and he accepted the living.

Wyndham's Acre
Probably the first clergyman to serve in the Church in the Square of 1838 was the Revd. Hugh Wyndham. He cultivated a plot of land at what is today Horseshoe Common, and this area became known as Wyndham's Common.

Wyndham employed a housekeeper, but for some strange reason they shared the only door key, so if both went out the key was left under the door mat to enable the first home to get in. One day a tramp gained entrance by using the key and stole Mr. Wyndham's silver. The tramp was caught and the silver recovered. The thief had to be walked to Winchester to serve his gaol sentence.

St. Peter's Organ
Thomas Burton, who was appointed organist to St. Peter's in 1869, told the story of how the vicar, the Revd. Morden Bennett, would not agree to a 'Viol D'Amour' stop on a new organ being built for the church. He considered this to be unsuitable for a church organ. However, the organist and the organ builders conspired to keep the stop but to label it 'Viol da Gamba'.

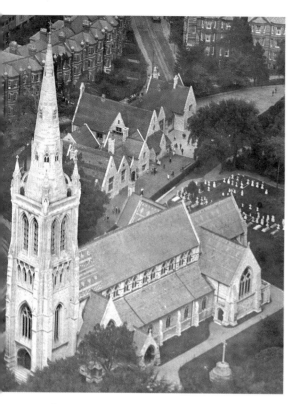

St Peter's Church, with its School at the north end which was pulled down to make way for flats, shops and up-market public houses.

The interior of St Stephen's Church.

Internally the church is rich and elaborate. The nave has painted Biblical scenes, there are alabaster pillars, and there is some fine stained glass by William Morris in the south chapel. The Twelve Apostles windows in the north aisle are a delight when the afternoon sun is shining through. The churchyard, with its Thirty Nine Steps (39 Articles of Religion) is also of interest as the burial place of Shelley's heart, his wife Mary Shelley, author of *Frankenstein,* and her mother, the feminist Mary Wollstonecraft Godwin, author of *A Vindication of the Rights of Women.*

The Chapel of the Resurrection by Ninian Comper (1925), in the south part of the churchyard, was used as a mortuary chapel to house the coffin prior to burial before funeral directors provided their own chapels of rest; ashes of the dead may still be kept here. It is also a War Memorial and is now used on Sundays by the Unitarian Church. The churchyard is maintained by the local authority as it is regarded as a 'lung' in central Bournemouth.

The Hon Grantly Berkeley wrote in the mid-19th century: '*It has often entered my head at Bournemouth, I suppose of course in opposition to the established fact, that in Bournemouth there could not be a den of thieves, as our clergy, good men at times, have made it their den . . . . they have so washed the site with holy water that sin ought to have fled and virtue become triumphant*'.

St. Stephen's Church (1881-1898), almost behind the Town Hall, was known in its early days as 'The Bennett Memorial Church', as it was built by public subscription to show gratitude for the indefatigable work of the first vicar of St. Peter's in establishing churches and schools throughout the town. The marble and stone-vaulted interior of St. Stephen's is inspiring, and the acoustics for choral singing are probably the best of any church in the country. It is generally regarded as being the best Gothic revival church in Dorset, and was famously described by Sir John Betjeman as worth '*travelling 200 miles and being sick in the coach to see.*'

Morden Bennett '*recognised a responsibility for the spiritual care and education of the people of the artisan suburbs*' that were springing up on the surrounding heathlands of the fledgling town.

He established eight churches: St. John the Baptist at Moordown, a church school founded in 1854, and better known as 'St. John in the Wilderness'. Today, it is referred to as 'Moordown St. John.' St. James', Pokesdown, (1858) was set amongst Admiral Popham's house and half a dozen small thatched houses on the north side of the Christchurch Road. Once again, G.E. Street was the architect.

St. Michael's grew from its school, and the present building on Poole Hill was designed by Norman Shaw, who was also responsible for the barn-like St. Swithun's (1876), now an evangelical church attracting large congregations.

St. Clement's (1871) was built on Boscombe Heath and is surrounded with houses in the area known as Springbourne. This report of the Bishop consecrating the building in April 1873, appeared in the press: '*The bishop will have given pleasure to the more Evangelical Churchmen of the Diocese from the fact that he would not proceed with the Service until the candles on the reredos were extinguished, and that he would not proceed with the Communion Service until the wafer was substituted by bread.'*

St. Ambrose at Westbourne began as a mission room in 1877; whilst outside Bournemouth were St. Aldhelm's at Branksome, and St. Barnabas at East Parley. A modern church of that name is now on a split level site at Queens Park.

The Punshon Wesleyan Church (1886) on Richmond Hill was destroyed by enemy action in 1943 and it was rebuilt in the modern style in Exeter Road in 1953.

The main Roman Catholic church of the town, the Sacred Heart, was completed and consecrated in 1900. It was run by the Society of Jesus for many years. Until very recently the parish priest was Fr. Murphy O'Connor, the brother of the Cardinal Archbishop of Westminster.

Richmond Hill United Reformed Church (1891) was regarded as the 'cathedral of congregationalism' as its ministers were always great preachers (Dr. J.D. Jones) and many of the church members took an active part in the affairs of the town.

Holy Trinity Church, (now demolished) Old Christchurch Road. It is easy to see why it was called the 'Rocket' church.

Anglican (31)

St. Alban, Charminster;

St. Ambrose, Westbourne (1900)

St. Andrew, Boscombe

St. Augustine, Cemetery Junction

Christ Church, Westbourne (1913, originally St. Nathaniel) is a Church Peculiar, having no parish of its own

All Saints, Southbourne

Holy Epiphany, Castle Lane

St. Andrew, Bennett Road

*St. Andrew, Kinson (Salisbury)

St. Barnabas , Queens Park

St. Mary, Holdenhurst Rd (redundant)

St. Christopher, Southbourne

St. Clement, Springbourne

St. James, Pokesdown

St. John the Evangelist, Holdenhurst

St. John of the Open Door, Boscombe

St. John the Baptist, Moordown (1875)

St. Katherine, Southbourne

St. Francis, East Way

Holy Trinity, Old Christchurch Rd (redundant, now offices)

St. John, Surrey Road

St. Michael, Poole Hill

St. Luke, Winton

*St. Mark, Talbot Village (Salisbury)

St. Mary, Holdenhurst Rd (redundant)

St. Nicholas, Hengistbury Head

St. Paul, Throop (formerly by the Central Railway Station)

St. Peter, Town Centre, Hinton Road

Punshon Methodist Church, Exeter Road, with the Bournemouth Eye in the background.

One Catholic

In 1863 there was only one resident Catholic in Bournemouth, Thorns Long. Later, to cater for the needs of visiting Catholics, private oratories were organised by well-to-do Catholics, usually in their own homes.

The alternative was a journey to Poole where a mission had been started in 1839. In 1868, through the generosity of Mr. & Mrs. Harnett, who were visitors from Ireland, a bus was provided each Sunday to take Catholics from Bournemouth to Poole. In the following year, a chapel was established in Bournemouth, the forerunner of the Oratory of The Sacred Heart on Richmond Hill.

St Paul's Church, Central Station

This was one of Bournemouth's 'low' evangelical churches. In the clergy stalls was printed a notice for all visiting clergy and Readers to note when they came to take a service in the absence of the vicar. *'Under no circumstances should you face the east when you say the Creed, nor should you cross yourself. Nor should you intone the Responses even though the choir sings them.'*

The now demolished church had a beautiful reredos but one of the vicars, a former Navy chaplain, had the whole of the interior painted battleship grey – including the reredos.

Society of Friends (Quakers)

The Society of Friends established a Meeting House in Avenue Road in 1872 for 90 worshippers.

In 1964, Marks and Spencer wished to enlarge their shop into the area occupied by the Meeting House. The firm offered to build a new Meeting House to the Friends' specification if they could have their space. The fine, purpose-built Meeting House is in Wharncliffe Road at Boscombe, and Lord Seif, then Chairman of Marks and Spencer, told its builders to skimp on nothing. 'I belong to a persecuted race, they belonged to a persecuted religion', he said.

St. Stephen, Town Centre, St Stephen's Road
*St. Philip, West Howe (Salisbury)
St. Saviour, Iford
*St. Thomas, Ensbury Park (Salisbury)

All the churches are in the Diocese of Winchester, except those indicated by * which are in the Salisbury Diocese. It is confusing to many people that there are four churches called 'St. John's', so they are always referred to by their geographical location: St. John's, Boscombe; St. John's, Holdenhurst; St. John's, Surrey Road; and Moordown St. John's. Similarly there is a St. Andrew's, Kinson; St. Andrew's, Boscombe; St. Andrew's, Bennett Road; and St. Andrew's Presbyterian in the Square, which closed in 2004.

Other Churches

Apostolic Church, Victoria Park Rd
Christadelphian, Winton
Christadelphian, Bath Rd
Christian Scientist, Christchurch Rd
Church of the Nazarene, Mayfield Rd
Elim Church, Hawthorne Rd & Curzon Rd
Evangelical Free, Howarth Rd
First Church of Jesus Christ of the Latter Day Saints (Mormon),
    Wimborne Road,
Howeth Rd Evangelical
Islamic Centre, St Stephen's Rd
Jehovah Witness, South Rd
Jehovah Witness, Elms Rd
Jehovah Witness, Millams Rd
Lutheran, Malvern Rd
Martin Luther Church, Moordown
Metropolitan Community, Hannington Rd
Orthodox Church of Joseph of Aramathea, Firbank Road
Orthodox Church, Osborne Rd & Woodbury Ave
New Church, Tuckton Rd
New Life Christian Fellowship, East Howe Lane
Salvation Army, Boscombe
Salvation Army, Winton
Seventh Day Adventist, Alma Rd
Society of Friends (Quakers), Wharnford Rd
Spiritualist, Bath Rd
Spiritualist, Charminster Rd
Strouden Park Chapel
Tuckton Christian Fellowship, Cranleigh Rd
Unitarian, Hinton Rd
Vineyard, King's Park School
Wessex Christian Centre, Hinton Rd
Winton Evangelical
Winton Evangelical. Hawthorn Rd

Roman Catholic

Annunciation, Charminster Road
Corpus Christi, Boscombe
Our Lady Queen of Peace, Southbourne
St Bernadette's, Draycott Road
St Edmund Campion, Castle Lane
Sacred Heart, Albert Road
Our Lady Immaculate, Westbourne
St. Thomas More, Exton Road

Free Churches

Boscombe Baptist
Iford Baptist, Old Bridge Rd
Lansdowne Baptist
Moordown Baptist
Roseberry Park Baptist, Boscombe
Westbourne Baptist
West Cliff Baptist
West Howe Baptist, Holloway Av
Winton Baptist, Cardigan Road

Kinson Methodist
Punshon Methodist, Exeter Rd
St. George's Methodist, Portman Rd
Southbourne Methodist,
Westbourne Methodist
Winton Methodist
Victoria Park Methodist

East Cliff URC, Central Station
East Howe URC
Immanuel URC, Southbourne Rd
Richmond Hill URC, Town Centre
Sutton Road URC
Throop URC
Trinity URC
Westbourne URC
Winton URC, Luther Rd

Hebrew Congregation

Orthodox Synagogue, Wootton Gardens
Reform Synagogue, Christchurch Road

St. Birinus Mission in Easter Road became the Luther Kirche in 1963. Sir Giles Gilbert Scott, the famous architect of the Anglican Liverpool Cathedral, designed the Roman Catholic Church of the Annunciation (1906) in Charminster Road.

The Eternal Flame powered by gas at a cost of £9,000 a year is paid for by the churches of the town. Behind it is the Camera Obscura and café.

Salvation Army Band, 1887

When a Salvation Army company was formed in Boscombe its music was provided by 4 cornets, a violin, a flute, a triangle and a drum.

In an issue of 1887, the *Bournemouth Guardian* praised the band's enthusiasm but doubted its playing ability, saying that if the Army wished to retain the goodwill of the residents they would have to restrain the ardour of the man with the big drum. The Band at Boscombe today is highly regarded all over the country.

Congregational Worship

The UR (Congregational) Church in Throop was built in 1828 as an independent chapel. It relied on visiting preachers, and a flag was hoisted to inform local people when a service was about to take place.

In the early days of Congregational worship in Bournemouth, lay preachers would come from Christchurch to conduct cottage services. The Revd. Daniel Gunn was a man of character and forthright in his views of the prerogatives of the ministry. He made it a rule that, while a lay preacher could conduct a service, he could not preach his own sermons but had to read a sermon written by a properly accredited minister.

The Bournemouth Arcade.

The Arcades

The Gervis Arcade is known today as the Bournemouth Arcade. It was originally begun in 1866 by the builder Henry Joy, who also built Southbourne Terrace and some villas near the Lansdowne. For a long time it was open to the sky, and was only finally roofed and glazed in 1873. Once, there were seats for those who wished to window shop or listen to the bands which performed there in a gallery at the east end at certain hours daily. Today, trios or quartets of music students, on regrettably rare occasions, perform classical music.

During the winter season the Arcade is the favourite promenade of the town. Without doubt, one of Bournemouth's most interesting sights is the motley concourse of fashion which parades in the Arcade on a wet or dull day, strongly reminding one of Bath in the days of the autocratic Beau Nash.

The Town Hall Avenue Arcade, known now as the Criterion Arcade, is opposite the Bournemouth Arcade and has now been converted from a dozen small shops of character into two large shops with its listed façade preserved. In former times prams were wisely banned from using this Arcade.

St. Peter's Walk

This is the part of Old Christchurch Road between the Bournemouth Arcade and the Criterion Arcade. Above it is a tall, wrought iron canopy and from its roof hangs an enormous watch, the gift of the people of Lucerne, Switzerland, which twinned with Bournemouth in 1981. As a contrast to the classical music played in the Arcade, jazz and pop music can occasionally be heard echoing under its canopy. The 'arch' appears to face the wrong way; this is because the appropriate officials at the Town Hall had to make sure that a fire engine could pass through unimpeded.

Conservation Areas

There are 21 Conservation Areas in Bournemouth and there is also a list of buildings that are worthy of being saved for future generations. Some form an important part of the life of the town. Not all are prominent, but

Conservation Areas

Boscombe Manor, Boscombe Spa, Churchill Gardens, Dean Park, East Cliff, Holdenhurst East, Holdenhurst West, Knole Road, Meyrick Park and Talbot Woods, Muscliff Lane, Old Christchurch Road, Portchester Road, The Saints, Southbourne Grove, Talbot Village, Throop Village, Undercliff Road, Westbourne, West Cliff and Poole Hill, West Overcliff Drive and Wick Village.

Church Glen

Church Glen was a beautiful valley lying between what is now St. Peter's Walk and Gervis Place. It belonged to Thomas Shettle, who also owned several houses in the Old Christchurch Road area. In 1851, for the convenience of his tenants, he built a rustic bridge across the glen to enable them to reach the sea more easily. The glen was about 20 feet deep and a small stream flowed through it on its way to join the Bourne Stream.

Henry Joy acquired the site in 1866, filled in the glen, and in its place built Gervis Arcade, better known as Bournemouth Arcade.

if they were to disappear for development or if they were drastically altered the town would be a poorer place. Even trees and garden walls can be protected, which, in the age of difficult car parking, can sometimes be a problem.

Residents of the town who have lived here for many years do not always know where these Conservation Areas are, so they miss seeing the glories of the Victorian and Edwardian past which would have disappeared if not protected. Already, hideous flat-roofed small blocks of flats have mushroomed to replace elderly villas in large gardens, and it is only in very recent years that the Planning Committee has insisted that the exterior appearance of the building should be pleasing and not necessarily built to the cheapest design for the maximum profit.

Bournemouth Council's Planning Department has produced an excellent series of booklets with colour photographs and exquisite drawings on each of the Conservation Areas.

The wrought iron Canopy at St Peter's Walk, Old Christchurch Road. (From the original watercolour by Mary How).

Listed Buildings

Listed Building status may be conferred on buildings to provide them with a legal protection against unauthorised alterations and to ensure that their character may be preserved for future generations. There are three Grade I buildings, the churches of St. Peter, St. Stephen and St. Clement. There are 225 Grade II listed entries in the town, of which three are Grade II* (St. Michael's Church Tower, The Russell-Cotes Museum, and The House of Bethany, formerly a convent next to St Clement's Church).

Recent Interesting Buildings

Some commercial buildings have used adventurous architecture, much to be admired. McCarthy and Stone's headquarters resembles an old-fashioned radio and, in the nearby Holdenhurst Road, the Unisys (formerly Abbey Life) building has an eye-catching, amusing, nautical look.

Three impressive buildings are on Richmond Hill. At the top, the 'space shuttle' – formerly Zurich, then Eagle Star, now First Start – appears to dominate the town even from the Bournemouth Eye. It is even more impressive inside with a central, glazed lift in an arboreal setting.

Further down the hill is the imposing, new headquarters of the Portman Building Society, and, doubtless to their chagrin, next door to it, is a stylish block of flats rising high. The *Daily Echo* building further down Richmond Hill, in the art deco style of the 1930s, has been declared a listed building.

On the Littledown Estate, are the gigantic greenhouse-style UK offices of Chase Manhattan, now JP Morgan, perpetually short of car parking spaces. Opposite it, in Castle Lane, is the new Bournemouth Hospital with its cheerful blue roofs of differing tints over different wards, apparently because the wrong coloured roof tiles were supplied for some sections that were built slightly later. It has 680 beds of which 344 are for general

House of Bethany
St. Clement's Industrial Home and Orphanage was founded in the 1860s next to the church to accommodate twelve poor girls who were to be educated and trained for domestic service. In 1872, three Sisters of Bethany came from London to take over the school, and a new orphanage for 100 children was built. A convent for the sisters opened in 1875, and an infirmary was added in 1897.

The orphanage suffered severe bomb damage in 1940, and could not be used again until 1950. In 1955, part of the building was adapted as a home for elderly ladies. In 1962, the Mother House moved from London to the Bournemouth House which was enlarged to accommodate them. The sisters have now left and the buildings have been converted to old people's flats. It is one of the most attractive developments in Bournemouth.

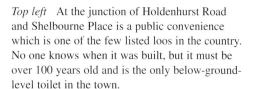

Top left At the junction of Holdenhurst Road and Shelbourne Place is a public convenience which is one of the few listed loos in the country. No one knows when it was built, but it must be over 100 years old and is the only below-ground-level toilet in the town.

Top Right The Littledown Leisure Centre, the second busiest leisure centre in the country.

Above McArthy and Stone's headquarters in Oxford Road, referred to by locals as the 'old radio'.

Above right Unisys, formerly the Abbey Life building in Holdenhurst Road. One of the joyful buildings of Bournemouth.

Right The new headquarters of the Portman Building Society on Richmond Hill.

medicine and 336 for surgery to serve a population of 317,000. This again is chronically short of car parking spaces.

Other eye-catching buildings in the neighbouring Wessex Fields are being developed for offices which boast two tall obelisks at either end. Beyond these are the Bournemouth Crown and County Courts, further offices and an hotel.

The new Bournemouth Library at the Triangle, a much overdue facility, is modern, attractive and has won a national award. It was built by Private Finance Initiative and will cost £66m over the agreed period, but this includes maintenance and caretaking charges. There is a paying car park opposite, expensive for the return of one book or to consult a reference book for a few minutes. There is no other convenient parking nearby, a drawback for many potential users.

There are also some unattractive buildings. The new Police Station in Madeira Road is forbiddingly bleak. Near it is an office building, monolithic with black glass and thus rather sombre. Then there is the Bournemouth International Centre. Two artists were commissioned to paint a picture of it for a client, but both refused because the building was so ugly. Fortunately, delegates like it because of its position near the sea and because the interior provides most of the facilities they require. It has been enlarged in 2005.

But the most unloved building in Bournemouth is the IMAX on the seafront by Bournemouth Pier. It has been vilified almost daily in letters published in the local press from the day it opened in 2000. It has even been suggested that it should be blown up!

Two enormous blocks of flats built just before the Second World War are still admired: San Remo Towers in Sea Road, Boscombe, built in the Spanish style; and Bath Hill Court built on the site of the former Vicarage of St. Peter's Church. In the early 1960s the Albany appeared in Manor Road with 134 flats on 17 floors. This and the unprepossessing Admiral's Walk (121 flats on 13 floors) at Westbourne both dominate their immediate surroundings. Green Park on the East Cliff is a more recent large development.

Above left A view from Bournemouth Pier looking east, with the Cloisters in the foreground. Behind is the Waterfront Centre containing the IMAX, and the Metro Palace Court Hotel.

Above The forbidding new Police Station in Madeira Road.

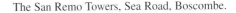
The San Remo Towers, Sea Road, Boscombe.

'Skerryvore', the house lived in by Robert Louis Stevenson between 1894-7. It was destroyed by enemy action in the Second World War.

Two views of Boscombe Manor, showing the house in 1906 and the inside of the Shelley Theatre (a listed building).

Blue Plaques

Each is arranged in alphabetical order of road, with location and date of unveiling. The words in italics are the actual words which appear on the plaque. Additional to these words on each are *'Borough of Bournemouth'* or *'Bournemouth Borough Council'*.

Alum Chine Road (61, Skerryvore. 1957) – tablet.
ROBERT LOUIS STEVENSON lived at Skerryvore overlooking this Chine from 1884-1887.

Avenue Road (Marks & Spencer, 1999)
Religious Society of Friends: QUAKERS. Bournemouth's Original Quaker Meeting House stood on part of this site for 82 years before being given to Marks & Spencer in 1964 in exchange for the present Quaker Meeting House in Wharncliffe Road, Boscombe.

Bath Road (Royal Bath Hotel, 1989)
1838 'BATH HOTEL'. Bournemouth's First Hotel built for Sir George Gervis, Architect Benjamin Ferrey. 1880 enlarged as 'Royal Bath Hotel' by Sir Merton Russell-Cotes.

Beechwood Avenue (Boscombe Manor, 1985)
BOSCOMBE MANOR. SIR PERCY FLORENCE SHELLEY. Son of the poet Percy Bysshe Shelley lived here from 1849 to 1889 and erected a private theatre in the building.

Bourne Avenue (Town Hall,1986)
TOWN HALL built 1881-85 as Hotel Mont Dore. Used during the First World War as a military hospital. Converted in 1921 to Town Hall.

Capston Road (No. 39. 1995)
39 Capston Road (since demolished). Home of FREDERICK CHARLES RIGG, V.C., M.M., Sergeant, 6th Battalion York and Lancaster Regiment. Born Springbourne 1888. Enlisted 1914. Killed in action near Epinoy, 1st October, 1918. Posthumously awarded The Victoria Cross for conspicuous bravery and resisting with his men to the last.

Capston Road (No. 175. 1995)
175 Capston Road, home of CECIL REGINALD NOBLE, V.C., Corporal, 2nd Battalion Rifle Brigade. Born here 1891. Enlisted 1910. Fatally wounded at Neuve Chapelle, 12th March, 1915. Posthmously awarded The Victoria Cross for conspicuous bravery in clearing barbed wire under severe fire allowing his battalion to advance.

Central Gardens (Pergola,1990) – Green Plaque
BOURNEMOUTH CENTENARY, 1890-1990. This Pergola has been created by the re-use of a Victorian cast-iron verandah rescued from

demolition during the construction of the 'Sovereign Centre' in Boscombe.

46 Dean Park Road (A plain plaque, 1975)
Here RUPERT BROOKE, 1888-1915, discovered poetry.

Derby Road (Langtree Manor Hotel, 1995)
Built 1877 as The Red House for the socialite, beauty and actress LILLIE LANGTRY 'The Jersey Lily' (1853-1929). Edward, Prince of Wales, (later King Edward VII) provided this residence to which he was a frequent visitor.

Douglas Mews (Stourfield House, 1994)
STOURFIELD HOUSE, 1776. These steps and the portico above, built in 1776 by Edmond Bott, were part of Stourfield House, later home to Mary Bowes, philanthropic Countess of Strathmore and ancestor of the present Queen (Queen Elizabeth the Queen Mother). Extended in 1898, the building became a hospital until its demolition in 1991. This replacement building was completed in 1993.

East Overcliff Drive (Hotel Miramar, 1992)
JOHN RONALD REUEL TOLKEIN, 1892 -1973, author and scholar, stayed here regularly from the 1950s until 1972.

Exeter Road (Site of 'Muriel', 1996) – Green Plaque.
The improved Terrace Road was officially declared open by the Chairman of the Highways and Works Sub Committee, Councillor Mrs. Jean Moore, on 29th April 1996 and this mosaic (sponsored by Tarmac Construction Ltd) represents a design by the artist AUBREY BEARDSLEY (1872-1898) who lived for some time in 'Muriel' the former house which formerly occupied this corner site.

Exeter Road (Royal Exeter Hotel, 1937) – tablet.
To the memory of LEWIS T.G. TREGONWELL who erected the first house in Bournemouth on this site in 1810. He died on Jan. 18th 1832, aged 73 and was buried in St Peter's Churchyard, Bournemouth. He was descended from Sir John Tregonwell a member of an ancient Cornish family. This tablet is erected by members of the Bournemouth and District Cornish Association and friends, Oct. 1937.

Gervis Road (47, Durlston Court Hotel, 1993)
Durlston Court Hotel was the childhood home of COMEDIAN TONY HANCOCK. His family moved here from The Railway Hotel, Holdenhurst Road. Tony's first engagement was entertaining the troops at the Sacred Heart Church on Richmond Hill.

Grove Road (57 East Cliff Cottage, 1996)
East Cliff Cottage Hotel, built 1895, was home to British actor James Stewart, better known as the film and theatre star STEWART GRANGER,

Lillie Langtry, favourite mistress of Edward VII.

The improved Terrace Road was officially declared open in 1996. This mosaic represents a design by the artist Aubrey Beardsley (1872-1898) who lived for some time in 'Muriel' a house which formerly occupied this corner site before its demolition for the road scheme.

The Waterworks at Iford Lane were used by Count Tchertkov to print the works of Tolstoy, the Russian writer. The area has now been converted into private houses.

1913-1993, notable for the films Scaramouche and Beau Brummell. His mother Mrs Lablanche Stewart owned this property until 1979.

Hinton Road (St Peter's Churchyard, north outer wall. 1995)
In this churchyard lie the mortal remains of MARY SHELLEY, author of 'Frankenstein'. Her father, William author of 'Political Justice'. Her mother author of 'The Rights of Women'. And the heart of Percy Bysshe, her husband, the poet.

Holdenhurst Road (2001)
Estcourt – 195 Holdenhurst Road. The final home of INSPECTOR FREDERICK GEORGE ABBERLINE (1913-1929). During his 29 years with the Metropolitan Police, Abberline gained commendations and awards and became well-known for his work on the case of Jack the Ripper.

Iford Lane (Iford Waterworks, 1985)
COUNT VLADIMIR TCHERTKOV & fellow Russian émigrés established the Free Age Press & Tolstoy's works were first printed here, 1900-1913.

Old Christchurch Road (1-3. 1987)
Site of 1857 iron 'SCOTCH' Church. Rebuilt in stone 1872. Present 'Central Chambers' built as three shops with club above by architects Lawson & Donkin, 1888. Then Mansion Hotel, Empress Hotel and groundfloor Cadena Café. 1920 became National Provincial Bank. National Westminster Bank, 1971.

Old Christchurch Road (Bournemouth Arcade)
BOURNEMOUTH ARCADE 1866 built by Henry Joy originally as two rows of shops. The glazed Arcade roof was added in 1872.

Old Christchurch Road (former Criterion Arcade, 1994)
TOWN HALL BUILDINGS 1875. Sir George Tapps built the thatched

'Ashley Cottages' here in 1812. In 1875 Bournemouth's first Town Hall was built on this site. The Civic Offices, which later became the Criterion Hotel, survive at the front, but with an 1898 façade at the front. The Hall was converted into an Arcade in 1886 and refurbished in 1962 and 1991.

8 Poole Road (2000)
'2 Westburn Terrace' formerly St. Aloysius School. PAUL MARIE-VERLAINE , 1844-1896. The French symbolist poet, after two 'dolorous' years in Belgium and France and a year teaching happily in Lincolnshire, taught French and Latin here, 1876-1877 and worshipped at the Church of the Sacred Heart in Bournemouth.

Post Office Road (Post Office, 1996)
BOURNEMOUTH POST OFFICE opened 1896. Bournemouth's First Office opened in 1839 at The Tregonwell Arms. After several relocations the office transferred to 'Beckford Place' (re-named Post Office Road about c.1900.) This centenary plaque was unveiled by the Mayor of Bournemouth, Councillor Mrs Jean Moore.

16 Richmond Hill (1998)
2 Richmond Terrace, which formerly stood on this site, was the birthplace of the musician HUBERT PARRY (1848-1918). Composer of 'Jerusalem', of the Coronation anthem 'I was glad' and of 'Blest pair of sirens'.

Richmond Hill, (Norfolk Hotel, 1988)
1840-1850 BUILT AS TWO LARGE VILLAS. 1870 Stewart's Hotel. 1903 enlarged with cast-iron verandah. 1910- Norfolk Hotel. Enlarged to 'Norfolk Royale' 1988.

Richmond Hill (Sacred Heart Church, 1993)
LADY GEORGIANA FULLERTON (1812-1885). A philanthropist, novelist and biographer lived from 1877 in Ayrfield, St. Peter's Road, Bournemouth. She founded St. Joseph's Convalescent Home and St Walburga's and worshipped at the Oratory of The Sacred Heart.

Richmond Hill (Granville Chambers, 1988)
1891 THE GRANVILLE CHAMBERS built as a temperance hotel by architects Lawson & Donkin. 1900-1930: Granville Hotel. 1930 used as offices. 1985: refurbished.

Richmond Hill (Walton House, 1992)
WALTON HOUSE built in 1861-62 by the newsagent William Henry Smith as his retirement home and named after his father Henry Walton Smith. W.H. Smith lived here until his death in 1865.

Somerville Road (St Michael's School, 1993)
FREDDIE MILLS, 1919-1965, World Light Heavyweight Boxing Champion was born at No 7 Terrace Road (since demolished) and

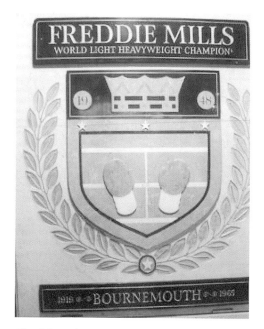

The Memorial to Freddie Mills, World Light Heavyweight Champion, is in the Littledown Centre.

attended St Michael's School. He trained in his converted garden shed and started boxing professionally at Bournemouth in 1936. He defeated Gus Lesnevich to win the World title on 26th June 1948.

South Cliff Road (Exeter Road, Court Royal, 1992)
COURT ROYAL formerly 'Madeira Hotel'. Notable guest Guglielmo Marconi built a 100 foot experiment aerial mast here and received the world's first paid radio message from Lord Kelvin on the Isle of Wight on the 3rd June 1898. Since 1947, Court Royal has been a convalescent home for South Wales miners.

Westover Road (Tourism Information Office, 1990)
To commemorate the original Information Bureau provided and operated by The Bournemouth Chamber of Trade 1928-1948).

Westover Road (Tourism Information Office, 1990)
Bournemouth's Tourism Information Centre opened by Lord Strathclyde, Minister for Tourism. 5th March 1990. Mayor: Cllr Harry Bostock.

Yelverton Road (Theatre Royal, 1987)
THE THEATRE ROYAL 1882. 1887 onwards used as Town Hall. 1892 – Theatre Royal. 1939 – Services Club. 1949 – New Theatre Royal. 1959 – Opera House. 1962 – Cinema. 1963 – Bingo Hall. 1985 – Curzon Casino Sporting Club.

ELEVEN

The Expanding Borough

Alum Chine

Alum Chine is about three quarters of a mile long and has at the sea end a fascinating Tropical Garden. There was an 'Allom House' nearby so it is likely that alum was 'myned' here as early as the seventeenth century. Development of the Chine was initiated by the building of 'Branksome Dene', which later was bought by Lord Wimborne, whose wife Cornelia was Winston Churchill's aunt. The Chine is famous as being where the young Winston jumped from a bridge in 1892 into the top of a fir tree, fell 29 feet, and was unconscious for three days. The history of the twentieth century might well have been very different had the accident been more serious.

There has been a refreshment cafe at the foot of the Chine for over a hundred years. The first proprietor was a Mrs. Stanley, who opened what she called a 'tin hut' in which she and her family lived. Tea and cocoa were heated on a paraffin stove. Mrs. Stanley extended the cafe, bought two bathing machines and hired a man and a donkey to pull them into the sea for easy and respectable bathing. One stormy night, a dead cow was washed ashore nearby. The next day the carcass was buried in the base of the cliffs. Years later, when the promenade was being built, the bones were excavated and an archaeologist was sent from the Natural History Museum to examine them as it was thought they were the remains of a prehistoric creature.

The owners in 1940 were given 48 hours' notice to pack up the cafe when beaches were closed and sea defences were erected because of the war.

Part of Alum Chine Tropical Gardens.

105

This photograph of the beach at Pokesdown in 1900 is obviously the Boscombe beach today. The building was used to house a band which gave occasional concerts.

The first Steps at Boscombe, known as '104 Steps Pokesdown'.

Boscombe

'*A place called Bastowe within the said Baye . . . at Bourne Mouth within the West Baye at Christchurch an easy place for the ennemye to lande*' is mentioned in the sixteenth century; and a Copperas House is known to have existed where ferrous sulphate or copperas was produced for use as a mordant in dyeing.

Much of what is now Boscombe was a furze and heath-covered common. Christchurch and a few houses at Pokesdown were the only signs of civilisation. There were tracks leading to Poole and one to the sea where the pier is now. By 1801, Boscombe Cottage had been built near Honeycomb Chine, on a site that later became the centre of the Boscombe Manor Estate developed by Sir Percy Shelley. A Boscombe Lodge existed and it became the property of Major Stephenson at an auction sale in 1841.

This was bought by Sir Percy Shelley in 1849 and it became successively known as Boscombe Place, Boscombe Manor, Groveley Manor, and Shelley Park. C.C. Creeke was the architect for the extension of the house and the theatre, over which, in 2004, there is such a public debate. Should it become an Arts Centre or be given over to housing? A medical centre is to be built there in 2006.

The main drive to the house connecting it to Christchurch Road is today's Chessel Avenue. A contemporary writer described the Lodge as 'being in the midst of plantations'. When plots of land were sold off for building houses, the materials could be found nearby: pleasant, red-coloured brick clay and wood from the plantations.

When Bournemouth Commissioners sought to include Boscombe there was an immediate protest from Boscombe residents, but this was overruled by the Local Government Board. An election for three seats to

The skeleton of a whale washed up on Boscombe beach in 1897 and finally assembled on the Pier to become a popular tourist attraction.

the Commissioners was held in 1876. The candidate who came bottom of the poll received only six votes.

The Duke of Argyll opened the 600 feet long Boscombe Pier in July 1889, followed by the traditional celebratory procession and dinner. Although intended for the growing number of visitors and used by a few paddle steamers, it could not compete with Bournemouth's popularity and its owners were relieved of a white elephant when the Council took it over in 1904. Its claim to fame was the display on its deck of a 65 feet long whale that had washed ashore nearby in 1897. After the flesh had rotted, children would slide on its larger bones until the novelty wore off, and its bones went to a business in Springbourne which ground them up and sold them for fertilizer. Nearly 100 years ago, the Chief Sanitary Inspector for Bournemouth reported that *'the event itself caused much trouble and the discharge of some particularly unpleasant duties'*. The pier is still there, awaiting its revamp in 2006.

There was religious controversy, of course. Services at St. Clement's Church (1873) were too 'high'. The Sisters of Bethany from London took over the school and orphanage, and today the site is used for attractive housing. A visitor from London felt *'that the existing churches did not provide the manner of worship'* which he considered suitable, so another corrugated iron church was built in Drummond Road, called Christ Church. A successful protest was made about the 'fever' hospital near the Water Tower being built as it was close to houses. It was closed to become the foundation of the Royal Victoria Hospital in Shelley Road, now flats since the transfer of the hospital to Castle Lane. The temperance movement was strong in the area and a Coffee Tavern was opened next to the Palmerston Arms.

Plots continued to be sold for large houses to be built upon, but there was still poverty in the area. Soup kitchens were opened and coal was distributed to the poor during the winter months. The Church of St. John was opened in 1893 with accommodation for 1,100 people and the first vicar was Revd. S.A. Selwyn, hence Selwyn Hall. St. George in the Woods was closed. St. Andrew's in Florence Road opened a chapel of ease in 1890, and the present building was consecrated in 1908. Corpus Christi

Boscombe Cliff Garden
The Cliff Garden was laid out by Lord Abinger in 1900 on six acres. Four years later, provision for bowls and tennis was introduced, and later a croquet lawn was laid.

Today, there is no provision for any game as, in 1924, a three acre slice of the cliff disappeared into the sea during a storm – which took the bowling green to the cliff edge. The site was left as grass until 1994 when an extensive conversion of the garden took place. Today, there is an arid garden of plants that thrive in any conditions, and an Italian garden with colonnades that support nothing.

Freemantle
Freemantle was the name of the area north of Christchurch Road between Wolverton Road and Pokesdown Station and northwards to the railway line. It became part of Bournemouth in 1884. The post office in the main road was, for many years, Freemantle Post Office, later to become Boscombe East Post Office.

Freemantle Hall in Somerset Road is the only reminder of the area today. This hall has existed for over 100 years, beginning life as a mission hall in 1885. Freemantle National School used the premises from 1896.

Boscombe Crescent Gardens with its Bandstand in the 1890s.

Roman Catholic Church (SJ) dates from 1896 with the then boundary between Boscombe and Pokesdown running through its site.

Gordon Boys' Home, near the Boscombe Post Office, was for orphaned and deprived boys and named after General Gordon of Khartoum. Between 20-30 boys aged 14-16 lived there, according to Edward E. Read's memories, and they wore a distinctive blue uniform and peaked cap. They earned their keep by doing odd jobs for people. Estate agents would employ them to erect or take down 'For Sale' boards.

The other important early development in Boscombe was the Boscombe Spa Estate between Boscombe Chine and Sea Road. The estate was developed by Sir Henry Wolff, MP for Christchurch, who built 'Boscombe Tower' in 1868 and laid out the surrounding land for private villas. It owed its name to a mineral spring on the east side of the Chine, over which Sir Henry built an open-sided thatched conical summer-house. Such was its medicinal reputation that local hotels proudly served jugs of the water at their tables as evidence of the healthy attractions of the area.

One such hotel, and the grandest, was the Boscombe Spa Hotel, which opened in 1874. The Hotel became Bournemouth College after six years,

The Spa at Boscombe was thatched as shown in this photograph of 1876. The Chine Hotel is in the background.

A Boscombe Hippodrome programme cover for 1929. The show was 'The Spice of Life – a splash of novelty with a flavour of fun. In seventeen scenes.'

and six years later it reverted to being an hotel which it still is: the Boscombe Chine Hotel. Plots were put on sale locally, but because it was a bleak place there was little interest in them until a development near Palmerston Road's inn, called The Ragged Cat, became popular. By 1871, 212 people lived in 19 houses in this area, of whom 70 people lived in just nine houses.

An early example of ecumenism took place in Boscombe in the mid-1870s. The Congregationalists (UR) joined with the Baptists; and the Boscombe British School was opened in 1878 for non-denominational Christian teaching under the stewardship of the Revd. H. Leonard. This movement was spoiled by the opening of the galvanised iron-clad St. George's in the Woods, another church with no pretensions to the High Anglicanism of St. Clement's. The present St. George's Methodist Church was built on or near the site.

Despite its hesitant start, Boscombe continued to grow, largely thanks to Archibald Beckett, who built both the Royal Arcade and Boscombe Theatre (Hippodrome) which were opened in the 1890s. Artisan houses were built north of the main Christchurch Road, and substantial marine villas on its south side nearer to the sea. Many of the houses between the two have been subdivided into flats and have become known as 'bed-sit land'. Although it may not be apparent from the outside, the area continues to harbour poverty and deprivation. At the end of the 20th century, the main road of Boscombe was pedestrianised and the large Sovereign Centre with a multi-storey car park was built. The fountain there has always been a controversial addition (see 1990 Centenary). More controversy has raged over whether the building of flats should be allowed at Honeycombe Chine on the sea front. The capital sum raised from the sale of the land would be used by the Council to improve the leisure amenities of the area in the hope that Boscombe would be rejuvenated.

Hengistbury Head

Hengistbury Head is a site of Special Scientific Interest, a Local Nature Reserve and a Scheduled Ancient Monument. Because of its outstandingly lovely views, its peace and tranquillity and its convenient nearby car park, over one million people visit it every year 'to get away from it all'. They may see the rare natterjack toad, the Dartford Warbler, 16 breeding species of dragonflies and any one of 500 different plant species recorded there.

The Head is known all over the world to those interested in prehistory.

Ironstone Production

In 1848, a Mr. Holloway formed a company to dredge ironstone from the sea at Hengistbury Head and to quarry it on the headland. The dredging was stopped after eight years as it was causing rapid erosion – about 10 yards a year being claimed by the sea. This continued to a lesser degree until a groyne was built in 1938.

The ironstone was of good quality: 30% iron. As Mr. Holloway was a coal merchant, he brought coal from South Wales in his lighters and these returned, loaded with ironstone for smelting. At Hengistbury, his ships loaded at Holloway's Dock which was situated in a lagoon off the river. It is now silted up. In 1976, the quarry was converted into a lake – Quarry Lake, which is popular with schoolchildren who go pond dipping.

Rabbits

A memorial was erected on Hengistbury Head to Charles Smith (1845-61) who was accidentally shot whilst shooting rabbits there. The monument was moved because of cliff erosion to the churchyard of St James' Church, Pokesdown, where it still stands.

Erosion

Near the seaward extremity of the Double Dykes at Hengistbury Head is a monument that has been moved inland three times during the 50 years since its erection, giving a loss of 150 yards in 50 years as the amount by which the sea has advanced, or an average rate of three yards per annum.
Royal Sanitary Institute Conference, Bournemouth, 1922

Snakebites at Throop

In the days when Bournemouth and its outskirts were still largely heath there was an abundance of adders. To combat snakebite, farmers kept a bottle of snakebite antidote in a hole made in gateposts. Anyone who got bitten knew where to look for the antidote. The last such gatepost was in Throop as late as the 1960s.

There are Upper Palaeolithic and Middle Stone Age sites from 12,500 to 7,500 years ago, when the coastline was much further south. Excavations in 1911-12 produced gold-covered cloak buttons and a necklace of amber beads from the early Bronze Age; also a gold bracelet of the Romano-British period. In the late Iron Age, just prior to the Roman invasion, it was an important port trading with Rome and continental Europe. Inside the Double Dykes, a great earthen bank fortification probably built to defend the port, there is evidence of hut circles and of smelting coins, a few of which have been found. The Beaker People of the early Bronze Age left evidence of their beakers at the Head and also in Boscombe, Talbot Woods and a few at Kinson. Four hundred ancient burials have been found in the Bournemouth area, and artefacts have been discovered in the ground all over the town.

For those who are not energetic walkers, there is a land train to see its beauties and to admire the ponds formed from mid-19th century open-cast mining of iron stone. For centuries the Head has been used for occasional non-intensive farming, and in 1991, hardy Galloway Cattle were introduced to enhance the breaking up of the soil for the easier seeding of plants. Fencing off part of the Head has led to the return of skylarks and meadow pipits. Hidden from public view is the Marine Training Centre, used by sailors and canoeists in the sheltered water at the Christchurch side of the Head. The south and the west of the peninsula are subject to strong waves and winds, and erosion is a constant problem.

An early *Guide to Southbourne* said that Hengistbury Head belonged to Sir George Meyrick and he allowed people to go there provided '*they keep to the beaten path and are without dog*'. It is estimated that 250,000 people a year now walk their dogs there (also top of the 'dislikes' in a survey conducted in the 1990s: the high car parking charges came second).

Holdenhurst and Throop

Bournemouth was in the civic parish of Holdenhurst until 1874, as boundary posts at Surrey Road and at Talbot Road still show. A map dated 1575 shows the village as Holenest, and records indicate that beekeeping seems to have been an important occupation there in addition to rush gathering and milling. Holdenhurst Mill, now called Throop Mill, had four brick kilns in the mid-19th century to supply the building of expanding Bournemouth.

The villagers contributed to the repair of the 'Bourne Plank' in 1743, the first reference made to a bridge in central Bournemouth, and for a time it was known as Holdenhurst Plank. Smallpox epidemics in the village seemed to be commonplace, and treatments by local doctors show that porter, rum, gin and wine were all prescribed as treatments between 1816 and 1822. A small, thatched 'Lepers' Hospital' exists in the garden of one of the houses looking on to the Green, but whether it served as such is open to doubt.

The present church of 1834 contains the font of a previous church on the site dating back to Norman times. A few years before the present

OLD POST OFFICE COTTAGES, THROOP. in 1944.

DAIRYMAN'S COTTAGE, MANOR FARM HOLDENHURST, in 1944. t

HOLDENHURST FARM, in 1945

Above This old marker stone on the main road to the University, Talbot Woods, bears the inscription 'Parish of Holdenhurst'. It is regarded more by dogs than by the thousands of people who pass it daily.

Left Three of the delightful drawings of farmhouses and cottages made by Kathleen M. Chilver for her book *Holdenhurst: Mother of Bournemouth* which she published in 1956. Today, no one knows of her existence.

Hadden Hill

Hadden Hill was a wooded estate of 20 acres lying to the south of Castle Lane in the Strouden area. Here, in about 1870, the Revd. Frederick Hopkins, the Vicar of Holdenhurst, built Holdenhurst Lodge for his own occupation and after his death by his son.

After the First World War, the estate was developed although the house remained. During the outbreak of typhoid in the town in 1936, it was used as an emergency hospital, but in the 1940s the Lodge was demolished as further development took place. The small house at the entrance to the drive is still used as a residence. It is on the corner of Castle Lane and Mount Pleasant Drive, the latter being originally the entrance to Holdenhurst Lodge. A nearby road bears the name Hadden, all that reminds us of Hadden Hill.

The Old Iford Bridge.

church was built, the 5th Earl of Malmesbury records that '*going to church at Holdenhurst was a service of such danger in the winter floods, that a bridge was subsequently built by the 3rd Earl for the purpose of connecting Heron Court with Holdenhurst*'. The house next to the church used to be an inn named The Three Elms, and another, The Jolly Sailor, was opposite the Mill.

Holdenhurst's rural isolation from the 'civilizing' influence of Bournemouth came to an end with the building of 'Holdenhurst Lodge' in the 1860s, whose owner was the vicar, Frederick Hopkins. The estate was broken up and developed after the First World War, and the house was demolished after the Second.

Iford

Iford, or Iver, was a well known ford with its little islands over the River Stour. The Old Iford Bridge is no longer used, but two of its five sections may still be seen. It was built in 1784 and the arches' bases rested on the different islands.

It is recorded that a shop in Iford was struck by lightning in 1822 and three persons in it were severely burnt. This pre-dates by 30 years the first shop in Pokesdown. Clinghan Charity Farm, on the site now occupied by Swanmore Rose Garden, was covered with large vines, and parts of the farm still existed next to 1357 Christchurch Road until well after the Second World War.

Kinson

Kinson was originally in the Rural District of Poole, in the County of Dorset, and it extended from Branksome and Newtown, through Boundary Road (Lane), and along Redhill. Its area went nearly to St. John's Church in Surrey Road, ended by the 'Parish of Holdenhurst' where a boundary stone may still be seen.

At the beginning of the 19th century when Bournemouth had only one building, Kinson boasted 96 and a population of 497, of whom 466 were agricultural workers and 23 were tradesmen. St. Andrew's Church is in

Above The Dolphin Inn (now Gulliver's Tavern), Kinson, from a 1921 postcard.

Left 'Pelhams' (1793) now extended and used by the Council as the Kinson Community Association. Further extensions were opened in 2005.

Millhams Lane and is famous for the grooves in its tower said to have been caused by ropes hauling up and down the barrels of smuggled goods, probably under the direction of the infamous Isaac Gulliver. The pub named after him in the main road was formerly called The Dolphin. The other pub is The Royal Oak built on the site of The Travellers' Rest.

There can be few local residents left who can boast of having changed their county address three times without having moved house. Kinson was originally in Dorset, but its Parish Council unanimously rejected the overtures of Poole to join it, and instead chose in 1931 to join with Bournemouth which was in Hampshire. In 1974, Bournemouth was put into Dorset under local government reorganisation. But the ecclesiastical boundaries remained unchanged and so St. Andrew's, St. Philip's, St. Thomas's and St. Mark's, Talbot Village, remained in the Diocese of Salisbury, the rest of Bournemouth being in the Diocese of Winchester.

Kinson can boast the second oldest mansion in Bournemouth: 'Pelhams', built in 1793 on land owned by Isaac Gulliver. It became the vicarage for St Andrew's Church when it was made independent from Canford Church. It was sold to the Council in 1931 by the Revd. A.M. Sharp on condition that it should be for community use and its land not built on. It is now a thriving Kinson Community Association (always called 'K.C.A.') with activities and classes taking place all day and every evening. More extensions took place in 2004.

The Village Green, with its modern stocks, only dates from 1967 when the former Kinson Primary School on that site was demolished. It survived

Unoffical Shoots
In the 1800s, an annual sparrow-shooting match was held on Boxing Day at the Dolphin Inn (now Gullivers) in Kinson. Before the event, boys would set traps for sparrows which they sold to organisers of the contest. This practice ceased in 1890 when an Act of Parliament banned the release of caged birds for shooting.

Until the 1960s, a group of men would occasionally meet just before daybreak at St. James Church, Pokesdown, then go to Bournemouth's Pleasure Gardens, armed with guns to shoot the grey squirrels which were causing great damage to the plants and bulbs. Council officers knew nothing of this cull, though Park Attendants were often surprised to find dozens of dead squirrels.

The Shoulder of Mutton
Mr. Atkins, the licensee of the Shoulder of Mutton, was the biggest man in Dorset; he weighed over 30 stones. When he died in an upstairs room the undertakers found they couldn't get his coffin down the stairs, so they had to take a window out and lower the coffin.

The Red Triangle Farm Colony was established by the YMCA in 1917 as a training farm for servicemen invalided out of the forces with tuberculosis. It was situated at West Howe very near the Shoulder of Mutton public house on the Ringwood Road. The men received instruction in the running of a smallholding. There was room for 24 in the colony, which closed in 1920.

Augustus John
The artist Augustus John used to take the gypsies of West Howe into the Shoulder of Mutton where he would treat them to beer and they would all sing songs together.

The Brickworks at Elliott Road near Ringwood Road/Turbary Park Road.

a disagreement in 20002/3 with the police authority who wanted to build a police station on most of the grass.

Kinson's main industries have been agriculture and brick-making, and potteries which moved from Bear Cross to West Howe for the better clay there. In recent times the main occupation has been in house building, especially to the west where large areas of social housing have been developed. Turbary Common, in the west of the area, is most like the original look of Bournemouth as it was in the early 19th century.

The only other reminder of the past is the old cedar tree near Avebury Avenue, which once stood in the garden of Ensbury House.

Northbourne has been in existence for about fifty years and is the name given to the housing development between Kinson and Redhill.

Muccleshell

'Big Hill' or 'Berry Hill' is an area little known today, although Muccleshell Cottages exist with that name. The Farm dates from 1587 and has an end wall nearly three feet thick. The 18th century house, with columns supporting its porch, was known for making ships' biscuits for the Poole-Newfoundland run, and the brick oven may still be seen today. The river view from Muscliffe was a renowned beauty spot and *Sydenham's Guide to Bournemouth*, published in 1890, extols it thus:

'Muscliffe – a charming spot, and which should form a principal object in the inland drive to the Stour valley. Leaving the carriage at one of the little wayside inns at the adjoining hamlet of Throop, a gully or slope to an old fording-place opens to the footpath and the winding course to the Stour is seen opening at the foot of a lofty bank or cliff, clothed with underwood and overhung and fringed at its summit with magnificent trees. At one part an alluvial flat lies between the wooded precipice and the river, and gives an exquisite site for a picnic. The visitor should follow this footway to the village which stands clustering its rustic cottages upon the banks further on; it is highly characteristic and a visit to these and other remote spots in the fertile valley of the Stour will be long remembered.'

Muccleshell Cottages, Holdenhurst, 1873.

Pokesdown

There is archaeological evidence that shows this part of Bournemouth was inhabited in the Stone and Bronze Ages, but until the mid-1700s it consisted of a farm and a few cottages. It 1766 a barrister and local magistrate, Edmund Bott, built Stourfield House, where '*he entertained some of the best men in the neighbourhood in a more intellectual fashion than was customary at other houses at that time.*' It later was bought by Sir George Tapps, followed in 1844 by Admiral Charles Popham. After the break up of the estate at the end of the 19th century it became part of Douglas Home Sanatorium and then Douglas House, part of the Dorset N.H.S. Trust.

By 1835, a small Congregational church had been built by its worshippers and enlarged in 1857 to accommodate all Free Church members in the area. The pleasing exterior design and other alterations were made in 1877, but it was sold for redevelopment in 2003. In the same year, St. James' School was opened, and a year later the church was dedicated.

By 1871 there was a population of 511 in Pokesdown compared with Boscombe's 207. Indeed, with its two pubs, school, chapel, church, blacksmith's forge and Mechanics Institute, it was the largest of the small communities growing up outside the area administered by the Bournemouth Commissioners. After a long, disappointing wait, the railway station opened in a deep cutting in 1886, but it was called Boscombe and not Pokesdown, which pleased the residents of neither. It was renamed 'Pokesdown (Boscombe)', and only finally became Pokesdown Station in 1897 when Boscombe Station opened in Ashley Road. The station was rebuilt in the 1930s, and largely remains unchanged.

Pokesdown Association, or Council as it became, applied to be incorporated in Bournemouth Council, mostly because the roads were in such a bad state, but it was not until 1901 that this took place.

Pokesdown

Shortly after Pokesdown became an Urban District Council in 1895, it was decided that the name of the village should be changed. Several suggestions were put forward and the residents were invited to vote on the following: Avonhurst, Boscombe Park, Havenbourne, Pinecliffe, Pinehurst-on-Sea, Portman Park, and Stonecliff.

Top of the poll was Pinecliffe with 199 votes, followed by Boscombe Park with 157. Fifty people voted for the name Pokesdown to be retained. They had their wish as the Local Government Board refused to sanction any change.

Slogan

The day after the Suez campagn began in 1956 there appeared on Pokesdown railway bridge this slogan: 'Empire Loyalists say be British not Yankee puppets'.

The words were crudely printed in 3 feet high letters in bright yellow paint, and are still faintly visible today.

Stourfield House

The first big house built in what was to become Bournemouth was Stourfield House at Pokesdown, built by Edmund Bott in 1766. The house stood in 450 acres, mostly laid out as parkland. There was a large greenhouse, a dovecote and an underground ice house. All that remains of the estate today is a road called New Park Road.

After Bott's death, there were several occupiers including the Countess of Strathmore, an ancestor of Queen Elizabeth The Queen Mother, who lived there from 1796-1800.

In 1893, the estate was sold and the house was used as a school. In the First World War it became the United Services Fund Hospital for service personnel who had a good chance of recovery, and was renamed Douglas House Hospital after Field Marshal Earl Haig.

In more recent years the building was as a hospital, but it closed in 1989 and was demolished to make way for housing. Only the fine front steps and portico have been retained, and now form the etrance to Stourfield Mansion.

The Redhill Tea Gardens in about 1900.

Redhill Common

Technically, it used to be in two counties and in two parishes: Kinson in Dorset and Holdenhurst in Hampshire, with the River Stour as a boundary. The river rights were controlled by Lord Malmesbury. The ford leading to West Parley by The Horse and Jockey was known as Riddlesford and there was an occasional ferry there.

That high part of the Common, which looks down on Wimborne Road, was known as Poors Common. It was covered in heath which, in turn, was covered by sheets and clothes spread out to dry by the many hand-laundries which serviced the hotels and guest houses in the town. It was also used for turf cutting for fuel, and cattle were grazed by those who were happy to provide milk for their own large family's needs. Eels were regularly caught or speared in the river, and hay and feed for horses was

The Stour at Redhill and its ferry

The Stour as it flowed by Redhill had many bends which were eroding the south bank and placing some houses in danger. In 1974 the Wessex Water Authority and the Council cut a straightened bed for the river a few hundred yards to the north to eliminate the bends. The old Ferry and Marshall's Riverside Tea Gardens site had to be filled in and the Caravan Park was allowed to extend over what was once the river. Tipping raised the area over which the pleasant walk now runs. The original Ferry was a punt which was pulled across by a rope. In later years a pole was used until it closed in 1934, in spite of petitions to keep it open.

The Horse and Jockey must have been a popular drinking place with those who lived north of the river. They would bribe the son of the owners of the Tea Garden and Ferry to take them across after closing time. No one suggests that these known numbers using the ferry were all late night drinkers, but 6,000 persons used the ferry in 1931; 8,000 in 1932; and a staggering 14,000 in 1933. It has always been a mystery why the rector of West Parley objected to the ferry there.

harvested and delivered to people in Bournemouth's town centre for those who had horses, which was nearly everybody.

A triumphal, turreted arch of evergreens over twenty feet high and fifteen feet wide was built by the villagers at Redhill to welcome the Prince of Wales when he visited the town in 1890.

Southbourne-on-Sea

'A favourite watering place & health resort for summer & winter'.

Dr T.A. Compton had great plans for a coastal area east of Boscombe which he was convinced could rival Bournemouth as a resort. By 1870 the Bournemouth doctor, who set up his practice four years earlier, had bought 230 acres with one mile of sea front and formed three companies for its development. Although a Southbourne Terrace of six shops with living accommodation above had already been built in Bournemouth, Dr Compton was determined to call his place 'Southbourne' because 'South' suggested warmth, one of the charms of the area.

By 1874, Compton had built a Winter Gardens about 320 feet long, bought second-hand, on the south side of Belle Vue Road and visitors were brought by carriage from Bournemouth to see the plants and flowers inside for 1/- (5p) return. *'Spend 5/- or more on flowers and vegetables and a refund of 6d from your admission will be given,'* was the popular gimmick. It was heated in winter by hot water and had originally been built for Mrs Assheton-Smith at Tedworth House near Andover by her husband, as a substitute for going abroad to a warmer climate for the sake of her health. An assembly room was soon built alongside to accommodate public meetings; but the Company was wound up in 1890.

Compton also saw to the building of a wooden Tuckton Bridge which opened as a toll bridge in May 1883. Prior investigations into the usage of the crossing had showed that the Wick Ferry accommodated 313 passenger movements daily and Iford Bridge carried 119. It proved to be

Southbourne
In *Picturesque Boscombe*, an illustrated booklet extolling Boscombe published in 1898, the following is written: *Southbourne has not prospered as might be expected . . . because its approach is somewhat second-rate, and those who have been responsible for the general development of the place have been unable to show their skill in the same substantive manner as those who are associated with the rise of Boscombe.*

Southbourne Pier in 1898. It was damaged by storms in 1900 and completely demolished by the Council in 1907.

Southbourne Terrace

The premises now occupied by W. H. Smith in the Square were built by Henry Joy in 1863 as a terrace of six shops with three storeys of living accommodation above. Mr. Joy called the building Southbourne Terrace several years before the district of Southbourne came into existence.

The Southbourne Cliff Bandstand and Lift

a financial success right from the beginning. The Council realised its importance to Bournemouth and bought it in 1904. Within a year, it was completely rebuilt to allow trams to cross it; but tolls were still charged until 1943.

Dr Compton was also ahead of Bournemouth by constructing an Undercliff drive, 1,740 feet long, which was opened in 1885 with the usual accompaniment of a public luncheon, a Regatta, flags, and a band to play popular selections of music. The doctor lived in one of the six houses built almost alongside it. Southbourne Pier, 300 feet long, was completed in 1888, before Boscombe's, and, from its first day of opening, pleasure steamers between Southbourne and Bournemouth operated. Twenty-four bathing boxes were for hire, but after a short time they were swept out to sea by a storm. Despite his belief in his new resort, Dr Compton had not taken into consideration the difference between the force of the winds in Southbourne and Bournemouth.

Nothing could combat the elements on the more exposed coast in this area: two French ships foundered nearby during the winter of 1898 and, by 1900, the pier had been battered to destruction. The row of houses which Dr Compton had so proudly built and lived in had been pulled down before the waves engulfed them and destroyed the undercliff. The sea

LIFF BANDSTAND & LIFT

encroached, Bournemouth Council took over the ruined pier in 1907, destroyed it completely for safety reasons and Southbourne-on-Sea is forgotten.

Left The six houses on the Esplanade at Southbourne, 1888. They were destroyed by storm damage shortly afterwards.

Above 137 Overcliff Drive, Southbourne, showing the remarkable Shell Garden created by George Howard between 1948 and his death in 1985. The Howard Centre at Christchurch Hospital named in his honour in recognition of the money the garden raised for charity remains his only legacy. The Shell Garden has now been demolished.

Talbot Village

In the mid nineteenth century, Georgina and Mary Anne Talbot bought 465 acres from Sir George Gervis and built a self-supporting village for unemployed workers. There were 16 cottages, each with one acre, and six farms permitted to sell only eggs, bacon, poultry and, later, homemade jam. But they had free grazing rights over 150 acres of heathland, where the Dorset Warbler and red squirrels remained common as late as the 1920s. Seven almshouses, designed by Bournemouth's ubiquitous C.C. Creeke, and a school were built in 1862, and the church in 1870. A special house was built for the church's organist.

The Almshouses, for the old and infirm of the labouring classes, were given rules by Miss Talbot, one of which was '*No inhabitant in Hampshire is to be admitted*'. (In those early days, Talbot Village was in Dorset.) The largest of the farms was later used by C.S. Rolls for practising flying prior to his death in 1910, and a Talbot Village aerodrome, opened in 1915, was called '*one of the finest private ones in England*'. It lasted for two years before transferring to Ensbury Park airfield.

White's Farm was so called because the buildings were painted white.

One of the cottages at Talbot Village.

Talbot Village

In the early days of the Talbot Village Almshouses, medicines prescribed for the tenants would be collected by the son of the school's headmaster. This involved his walking to and from Richmond Hill where the nearest dispensary was. For this service he received one shilling a week from the Trustees.

When St. Mark's Church was built at Talbot Village by the Misses Talbot, it had been intended that the tower should have a peal of bells. Someone suggested that the ringers would spend their payment on beer, so the Talbots had a change of mind and installed mechanical chimes that played a different tune each day, four times a day.

Westbourne

Westbourne was never an urban district with well defined boundaries like Boscombe, Winton and Pokesdown. It lays claim to one famous person who lived there for a short period, Robert Louis Stevenson, eight listed buildings and an excellent shopping centre of small shops, including a privately owned butcher, all within a compact area.

It had a rail connection to Poole in the early days at Bournemouth West, which was not linked to Bournemouth East (Central) until 1886. Bournemouth West finally closed in 1965, the station buildings were later demolished, and much of the site is now beneath the Wessex Way. Only the old Midland Hotel survives as a reminder of the station's links with the Midlands and the North, particularly through the famous 'Pines' Express which ran from Manchester to Bournemouth.

Branksome Tower, built by Charles Packe, MP for South Leicestershire, had the Avenue as its drive. Packe built the house in 1855 at the heart of what is now Branksome Park, and its lodge became County Gates, where the Dorset/Hampshire borders met. The surroundings of the Lodge may now be seen near the tennis courts of Branksome Chine. A plaque stands in a garden on the border of Bournemouth and Poole behind Waitrose car park *'to commemorate the creation of the two new Unitary Authorities on 3 April 1997'*. A transformer box used when there were tramways stands near Wessex Way and Frizzel House (now Liverpool Victoria) which is a most attractive, modern building standing on an enormous traffic island.

Zetland Court, Alumhurst Road, named after a prominent freemason, was formerly a convalescent home for Jewish ex-servicemen, and, prior to that, a vegetarian hotel. Herbert Home, was named after Sydney Herbert, who consulted his great friend Florence Nightingale over its design.

Churchgoing seemed to be popular in the area. The Nonconformists often initially worshipped in small, unprepossessing corrugated shacks,

Westbourne's architectural heritage ranges from small marine villas to old furniture depositories, the latter of which has recently been converted into flats.

Zetland Court

In 1860, Charles King purchased 40 acres of land in the Branksome Dene area from Robert Kerley and had a house built which he called Branksome Dene Hall.

By 1880 the estate had been acquired by Lord Wimborne and 'Hall' was dropped from its name. The Prince of Wales (later Edward VII) was a guest at the house when he came to Bournemouth to open Westbourne Hospital.

It passed into the hands of the Cassels and the Mountbattens and, in 1934, it was converted into a vegetarian hotel. During the War it was occupied by the Department of Education and then by Canadian troops. In 1950 it was briefly converted into 16 flats, but in the following year it became a Jewish convalescent home.

In 1983 the property was acquired by the Royal Masonic Benevolent Institution as a retirement home for Freemasons. The house was renamed Zetland Court after the second earl, who had been the Grand Master of the Institution in the late 1800s.

but by the start of the 20th century there were Baptist, Congregational and Methodist Churches which are still in use today. Henry Joy, who constructed the Arcade in 1884, built an Assembly Hall attached to it. From 1889, this was used by a breakaway Anglican church who named it The Church of the Holy Spirit, later known as St. Nathaniel's. This sect was legitimised in 1907, and by 1913 it had built Christ Church in Alumhurst Road; it is a church without a parish and is completely self-supporting from the collections given by its congregation. The Roman Catholic Church of Our Lady Immaculate now occupies the original Assembly Hall. St. Ambrose Anglican Church was opened in 1880 on land given by Cooper Dean.

Bournemouth's great arcade builder, Henry Joy, built another at Westbourne, where he lived. His name is commemorated by an inscription on the inside arch at each end: *'Westbourne Henry Joy's Arcade, 1884'*. The rainwater from the roof is carried via the drainpipes at the side of each shop into a channel which runs underneath the centre of the tiled paving – paving which once boasted a different pattern for each shop in the arcade.

By 1911, large villas for professional people had been built along Poole Road between Grosvenor Road and St. Michael's Church. Within a short time, 14 doctors and four dentists were practising in this small stretch. The Grand Cinema had 'a sliding roof to let the fug out', and it originally had an illuminated globe high on the roof. It became a bingo hall in 1977.

Westbourne Arcade designed by Henry Joy, 1884. His name is commemorated high up above the interior entry arches.

Left Wick Village, a country oasis at the east of Bournemouth, and *below* Wick Ferry.

Wick Ferry

The ferry was operated by the Miller family for 100 years until 1903. The fare was a halfpenny each way although Wick residents could travel back free of charge. Before 1863, when Tuckton Bridge was opened, the ferry was the only way to cross the Stour to Christchurch without going to Iford Bridge, a three mile detour.

Near to the ferry is the thatched Riverside Cottage. In 1815, it became the home of William Guard, chief bosun on Nelson's *Victory*. His granddaughter lived there until her death in 1982 at the age of 85. She had a pet monkey named Anna which she would take out on a lead. When Anna died, a memorial seat with a plaque was placed near the cottage. The plaque read, 'In memory of Anna'. Vandals destroyed it and it has not been replaced.

Winton and Moordown

A vote was held for the forming of a Parish Council in December 1894. Two painters, two builders, three carpenters and four other businessmen were amongst the eleven elected. There were fewer than 1,200 electors. Meetings were held at a house in Wycliffe Road and later at St Luke's School. It was not long before they protested to the District Council about the accumulation of surface water by Peter's Hill on Wimborne Road. They also at first refused to take responsibility for the lighting in the parish, but, when they did, the 45 lamps, which burned in the winter, were lit by oil. Lighting then ended on May 7, after which they were stored in a Mr White's loft until the nights began to draw in and they were brought out again on September 17. By 1896, mains water and gas had been laid in the area.

When Bournemouth Borough wished to take over the Parish of Winton, a solicitor was engaged to fight the proposition. Most people were '*artisans and workmen*' employed in the borough, but they knew that the undeveloped parts of the area, known as Talbot Woods and the Dean Estate, were likely to become valuable for building purposes. This explains why much of what people think of as Winton is in the Electoral District of Talbot Woods.

The residents of Moordown thought they had been overlooked by Winton in this decision; so they held their own meeting, and then informed Hampshire County Council that they had no wish to be included in the urban council, but should be transferred into the Parish of Holdenhurst. This wish, however, was not unanimous.

The Chairman of Winton Urban District Council became, ex-officio, a member of the bench of Magistrates in Bournemouth. The Council were asked '*that measures be taken to suppress the prevalence of bad language*'. They also asked the railway company to build a line to include Winton and told the Post Office they considered the present arrangements for collection of mail to be inadequate.

The supply of water in Moordown was also inadequate, so Winton

---

Look Up!

Turn up Cardigan Road from the Wimborne Road and look to your left as soon as you have passed the shops.

By an upstairs window on a private house is a concrete head surrounded by a white painted square. It is thought this is of a local builder named Charles 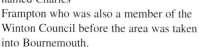 Frampton who was also a member of the Winton Council before the area was taken into Bournemouth.

The Victoria Chapel

This will be remembered by those who went into the garden of the 'Queen Vic' Hotel in Wimborne Road, which was then opposite Withermoor Road. The wife of the licensee of the time, Mrs. George, made a tiny chapel holding nine people from a static water tank, four pillars and a roof which were decorated with sea shells set in a thin layer of concrete. The inside was covered with pieces of broken pottery and there were stained glass windows. The statue of the Virgin Mary and the Bible were given in memory of a Canadian pilot killed in the Battle of Britain.

Dr. Loakes remembers

'In the days when Winton had its own telephone exchange and I wanted to go out for the evening, I would phone the exchange and leave a message. 'I shall be at telephone number 1234 tonight.' 'That's fine, doctor. I'll give you a ring there if a call comes through for you. Enjoy yourself'. This would be in the 1960s.'

Early Winton, 1872

It was reported that nearly 1,000 of the 'labouring classes' lived in Winton. When the Winton Urban District Council first sat in 1896, the first request was for improved Police protection and '*that measures be taken to suppress the prevalence of bad language*'.

Pascoe Marshall in his memories writes, 'He told me that the bricks he used (to build his house) he had collected a few at a time on his way home from work. All deliveries of bricks then, and for many years after, were by two-wheeled hand-carts and, owing to the rough state of the roads, some would always be falling off.'

Pascoe's grandparents lived in a cottage at Moordown and his grandfather planted holly trees by the gate and called the place 'The Hollies'. Hence the Hollies pub, which, discarding history, mysteriously changed its name overnight in 2003 to The Holly Tree.

Wimborne Road, Winton, in the early 1900s.

agreed to supply it with 244 gallons supplied by horse and cart three times a day.

Moordown was essentially agricultural land centred round the Malvern Road area. The old St John's building opposite The Holly Tree was once a chapel/school before St John the Baptist was consecrated in 1874. It then became a builder's merchants and is now part of a housing development.

A traffic census, taken on the Wimborne Road on a single summer's day in 1899, showed it was used by the following: 791 four wheeled vehicles, 1727 two wheeled vehicles, and 2827 pedestrians.

The Council agreed that the Tramway Company's intention to lay rails to Winton should be supported, provided the early morning and evening services would be at half-price for the benefit of working people. Yet they turned down a report for rubbish disposal as too expensive; households should be able to dispose of their own!

Discussions began again about Winton becoming part of the County Borough in 1901. Additional street lighting would be provided. As that seemed to be a main concern, agreement was reached.

When the landlord of the Queen Victoria Hotel, then in Wimborne Road opposite Withermoor Road, applied for a renewal of the licence, the magistrates said they had no complaint about the running of the hotel, '*but the population the landlord had to deal with was a very peculiar one*'. The hotel was demolished in the 1980s to make room for more shops.

Moordown Plane Crash
In the early hours of the morning on 21 March 1944 a Wellington bomber crashed on to Meadow Court flats just opposite the Hollies Inn (now The Holly Tree) in Wimborne Road. The plane was on a flight to North Africa and it had sustained mechanical failure. The eight man crew and two civilians were killed. The fire could be seen miles away.

TWELVE

Bournemouth People

What follows is a list (doubtless incomplete) of famous people who were born in Bournemouth or who lived or stayed in the town. It does not include those who came here for a short holiday, joining the many hundreds of thousands of people annually attracted to the town.

People associated with Bournemouth

Inspector Frederick ABBERLINE was the police officer in charge of the infamous Jack the Ripper murders, which took place in Whitechapel in 1888. He retired to Bournemouth in 1892 to live at 195 Holdenhurst Road, and died in 1929.

Thomas ALLAWAY was hanged in 1922 for the murder of Irene Wilkins in Iford Lane. His crime is known as the Decoy Telegrams Murder and has been the subject of various television documentaries. Was he really the guilty person?

Christian BALE was a pupil at Bournemouth School. He starred in the films *Empire of the Sun* and *The Matrix*.

Donald BAILEY lived in Southbourne. He designed the Bailey Bridge which was developed at the Experimental Bridging Establishment in Christchurch in 1941 and used with great success in the invasion of Europe. He was knighted in 1946.

Kenneth H. BAILY was the unofficial England cheerleader for nearly every international sporting occasion in the last 20 years of the 20th century. He always appeared dressed in a John Bull outfit and a top hat with a Union Jack on it. He wrote the Genevieve gossip column in *Bournemouth Times* and attended every local school sports day.

Dudley BARKER attended Bournemouth School in the 1920s and trained as a reporter on the *Daily Echo*. He wrote crime novels under the name of Lionel Black and became an associate editor of the famous magazine *John Bull*.

Vernon BARTLETT was at school here and later became a well-known writer and journalist in the 1930s.

Edward Wedlake BAYLEY (1773-1854) lived in the town towards the end of his life. He wrote *The Beauties of Wiltshire* and *The Beauties of England and Wales* in 15 volumes.

Aubrey BEARDSLEY lived between 1896 and 1898 at Muriel, on the corner of Exeter and Tregonwell Roads, now demolished. A lovely mosaic

---

Honorary Freemen

The Borough has awarded 23 men the title Honorary Freeman. They include the Commander in Chief of HM Forces in the Boer War, The Rt Hon Earl Roberts of Kandahar, Pretoria and Water-Ford, VC, PC, KP, GCB, GCSI, GCIE, DCL, LLD; an Admiral of the Fleet, Lord Beatty; and the Commander in Chief of HM Forces in the First World War, Earl Haig. The rest have been local people.

The Hampshire Regiment in 1945 and HMS *Phoebe* in 1988 have been granted the right to march through Bournemouth on all ceremonial occasions with colours flying, bands playing, drums beating and bayonets fixed.

Telephone Number One

When Mr. J.E. Beale had a telephone installed in his Fancy Fair, the number was Bournemouth One. But this was not the first telephone to be installed in the town. Bournemouth One was originally allocated to a local guest house and Mr. Beale acquired the number for the sum of ten pounds and the replacement of all the guest house's stationery.

based on one of his famous black and white drawings has been placed there. He was a prolific contributor to *The Yellow Book*, and he designed the first production of Wilde's play *Salome*. Some of his drawings were regarded as pornographic, even in the 1970s when they were published as posters. He died at the age of 25.

Charles BENNETT was Britain's first ever Olympic gold medallist when he won the 1500m in 4 minutes 6 secs and a team Gold in the 5,000m at the Paris Games in 1900. He worked as an engine driver in Bournemouth and on his retirement ran the Dolphin (now Gulliver's Tavern) in Kinson.

Tony BLACKBURN is a well-known disc jockey and broadcaster.

(Sir) Anthony BLUNT was the son of a Vicar of Holy Trinity Church. He became Keeper of The Queen's Pictures until it was discovered that he was one of the 'Cambridge' spies with Guy Burgess and Donald Maclean.

BLUR: Alex JAMES, a member of the pop group Blur, attended Summerbee School.

Guy BOOTHBY (1867-1905) was born in Australia but he lived for many years in Bournemouth in Watkin Road where he died. He wrote over 50 novels, many on Australian life, and his Dr. Nicola stories were very popular.

Phyllis BOTTOME (1884-1963) was the daughter of an American curate at St. Peter's Church, opposite which they lived. She became a popular novelist between the wars. *Search for the Soul* gives a glimpse into the life of Bournemouth and at St. Peter's.

Rupert BROOKE often visited Bournemouth. He was highly regarded as one of the World War One war poets and *'If I should die, think only this of me . . .'* turned out to be prophetic, as he died on the way to the Dardanelles at the age of 28.

Bill BRYSON, formerly a sub-editor on the *Bournemouth Daily Echo*, is a best-selling author of books such as *Notes from a Small Island* and *A Short History of Nearly Everything.*.

Frank Thomas BULLEN (1857-1915) died in Winton. He was a sailor who wrote books on the sea, the most famous of which was *Cruise of the Cacholet*.

Max BYGRAVES, the well-known entertainer and singer lived in Bournemouth until he moved to Australia in 2003.

Lord CAIRNS, a retired Lord Chancellor, lived at Lindisfarne, Manor Road, from 1873 until his death in 1885.

Roy CASTLE (1932-94) was a famous entertainer and TV star who lived just over the border in Canford Cliffs.

CHANG Woo Gow (1846-1893) was eight feet tall and lived with his family for the last three years of his life in Southcote Road. He was buried in Bournemouth Cemetery, but no trace of his grave remains.

Cumberland CLARK was a prolific author and poet, his works included *The Bournemouth Song Book* which is quoted in this book. He was killed in an air raid in 1941 and he left instructions that he should have an elaborate grave rather than that his money should be spent on a motor car.

Sir James CLARK was in practice in the town with his father. He went

---

Aubrey Beardsley

'Muriel' was a house which people said could not be built on the space available between Exeter and Terrace Roads. But it was, and was used for apartments, the HQ for a Ladies' Club, and, more famously, as where Aubrey Beardsley stayed from 1897.

It has now been demolished and a beautiful mosaic of a drawing by this famous illustrator to the *Yellow Book* may be seen there. A few months after he left Bournemouth for France in 1898, he was dead.

Joseph Cutler, who built the house and was one of the town's great characters, wrote: *'I would take the liberty of thanking all those who have hurled at me the thunderbolt of persecution, the lightning flash of falsehood, and the showers of slandering malice, and the mountains of damage I have sustained through this undertaking. He is mad for he is going to try and build a house where there is not room to stack a pile of bricks'.*

Paul Burrell

Paul Burrell, butler to Princess Diana, worked for a time at the Wessex Hotel on the West Cliff as an hotel assistant manager. In his book *A Royal Duty* he writes, *'Bournemouth went from bad to worse . . . I had no friends and was going nowhere'*. He hated every moment of his time working at the hotel (then under different management) having to serve as a storeman, waiter, and breakfast chef.

War Songs of the Allies

'Let the bombs bounce round about us,
And the shells come whizzing by,
Down in our air-raid shelter
We'll be easy, you and I.'
Cumberland Clark

Robert Day, Photographer

Robert Day was Bournemouth's first professional photographer, and it is from the many hundreds of negatives he left behind that we are able to see what early Bournemouth looked like. He arrived in 1862 and set up a small studio in a hut next to the Scotch Church in the Square. He was joined in the business by his son and his daughter, Harriet. An early advertisement for his studio included the footnote: *Ladies' and Children's Portraits are taken by Miss Day, if preferred.* Harriet specialised in portraits of children, winning several national awards before emigrating with her husband to New Zealand in 1883. The business continued until 1920.

Charles Darwin

Darwin didn't think much of Bournemouth: *'This is a nice but barren country and I can find nothing to look at. Even the brooks produce nothing. The country is like Patagonia.'* During the family's stay, one of Darwin's children and his wife developed scarlet fever.

Cliff Cottage, West Cliff, 1863, where Charles Darwin stayed in 1862. The Regent Palace Hotel was built on its site.

on to become Physician to Queen Victoria.

James CLAVELL, author of *Shogun,* was one of the Taunton School pupils evacuated to Bournemouth School during the Second World War.

Natalie CLEIN, won the BBC Young Musician of the Year in 1994 playing the cello and then became the first British winner of the Eurovision Young Musician of the Year. She attended Talbot Heath School.

Sir Alan COBHAM (1894-1973) lived at West Overcliff Drive. He was the first to fly to 17 different countries, and in 1926 he made a 27,000 mile round trip to Australia, for which he was knighted. He founded Flight Refuelling in 1934; and a lecture theatre in Bournemouth University is named after him.

Arthur COMPTON-RICKETT lived in Manor Road. He wrote *A History of English Literature*, well regarded in the 1930s.

Italia CONTI (1873-1946) began the famous stage school still flourishing in her name. Noel Coward was one of her early students. During the war she brought the school to Southbourne where she died.

John CREASEY (1909-73) lived in Bournemouth for 20 years. He wrote 560 novels, mostly crime thrillers, using 26 different pseudonyms, of which J.J. Marric, Jeremy Yorke and Michael Halliday were the most well-known. He could write a complete book in one week. He married his fourth wife a few weeks before he died.

Rupert CROFT-COOKE (1903-78) wrote 24 volumes of what has become the longest autobiography in the English Language. He was also a novelist and playwright. He lived the last five years of his life in Bourne Avenue.

Frank Leslie CROSS, a pupil of Bournemouth School, became Lady Margaret Professor of Divinity at Cambridge and he was the author of theological books.

Robert CRUIKSHANK began as a reporter on the *Bournemouth Guardian*. He became editor of the *News Chronicle*, the national daily newspaper.

John Nelson DARBY (1800-82) died in Bournemouth and was buried at Wimborne Road Cemetery. He founded the Plymouth Brethren sect and later he led the Exclusive Brethren.

Charles DARWIN, author of the influential *Origin of the Species,* stayed in 1862 at Cliff Cottage on the West Cliff.

Benjamin DISRAELI (1804-81), British Prime Minister and novelist, stayed at the Royal Bath Hotel for three months to relieve his gout on the advice of Queen Victoria. He was Prime Minister at the time and three Cabinet Council Meetings were held at the hotel.

Dai DOWER who came to live in Bournemouth in 1956 and taught PE at Ringwood Grammar School was Fly Weight Boxing Champion of Britain, Europe and The Empire.

Gerald DURRELL (d. 1995) was a zoologist and writer of popular books, largely about his experiences with animals. He tried unsuccessfully to open a zoo in Bournemouth and his sister, who lived here, kept many animals he sent her in her garden. He eventually opened a zoo in Jersey.

John EGLINTON spent a short time here. He was mentioned in James Joyce's *Ulysses* and was himself a writer on the Irish literary scene.

Ron EMBLETON (1930-87) lived in Carberry Avenue, Southbourne. He was regarded by many as one of the best strip cartoonists of the 20th century: the *Life of Ben Hogan*, cartoons for the Beaverbrook Press, *Biggles*, *Stingray*, *Captain Scarlett* and many well-known pretty girls for different publications.

Sir David ENGLISH, a pupil of Bournemouth School, became Editor of the *Daily Mail*. A local sports centre is named after him.

Eric EVANS was a curate at St. Peter's Church when he founded the local branch of the Samaritans. He later became Dean of St. Paul's Cathedral.

Eric FERNIHOUGH, a famous speedway rider, lived in Stourwood Avenue. He was killed in 1938 whilst attempting to break the world motorcycle speed record. He is buried in the Central Cemetery.

Benjamin FERREY was involved with the planning of early Bournemouth. The lithographs of his designs exist but they were never acted upon; but as they are published many believe, erroneously, that early Bournemouth looked like them. He wrote a standard work on Christchurch Priory.

Lady Georgiana FULLERTON (1812-85) was a Roman Catholic philanthropist who did much to develop the Church of the Sacred Heart, Roman Catholic education in the town (St. Walburga's, then in Yelverton Road), and St. Joseph's Convalescent Home. Nationally, she was known as an author.

John GALSWORTHY (1867-1933) attended Saugeen Prep School on the East Cliff and sang in St. Swithun's Church Choir. His novel, *The Forsyte Saga*, was memorably adapted for television. His plays, *Strife* and *Justice*, were powerfully influential and successful in the early part of the 20th century.

William GLADSTONE (1809-98), British Prime Minister and a masterly speaker, was buried in Westminster Abbey. As he left Bournemouth after a holiday he made his last public speech at the railway station. A plaque in St. Peter's Church is fixed to the lectern side choir stalls recording that he made his last communion in the church, sitting at that place.

Richard GODALL became a conductor at the Royal Opera House.

William GODWIN (1756-1836). His *Enquiry Concerning Political Justice* brought him fame and wealth. He married Mary Wollstonecraft and their daughter married the poet Shelley. He is buried in St. Peter's churchyard.

Jane GOODALL, the world authority on apes and campaigner for peace, attended Talbot Heath School and lives on the West Cliff. She was made a Dame in 2004.

Stewart GRANGER , the famous film star, lived in Bournemouth and a blue plaque has been erected in his honour at 57 Grove Road, East Cliff.

Charles GRAY, a member of the Bournemouth Little Theatre Club, became a professional actor and played in some of the Bond movies.

Lady Georgina Fullerton

The impression is often given that the early residents of Bournemouth were all wealthy, yet Lady Georgiana, a prominent Roman Catholic, wrote in the 1870s:

'This place is full of sorrows and sad destinies. It would be depressing but for the opportunities it gives of perhaps doing a little . . . and now there is an Irish family in a shed on the common without anything – five children ill with measles – mother dead. I am going to drive there this afternoon. But it is just as bad in Bournemouth as in London.

She started St. Joseph's Convalescent Home in Madeira Road where the new Police Station is now.

Gladstone

This great Victorian Prime Minister, who came to Bournemouth to recover from an illness, was told that his end was inevitable. But his desire was to die at home. The news that he was leaving Bournemouth 'spread abroad the town'. When he reached the railway station there was a crowd awaiting his arrival. Someone called out, 'God bless you, Sir'. Instantly he turned and, facing the crowd, lifted his hat and, in the deep tones which men knew so well, said, *'God bless you all, and this place, and the land we love'*. This benediction was Mr. Gladstone's last utterance in public.

Sir James GRIGG attended Bournemouth School. He was Secretary of State for War, 1942-45.

Isaac GULLIVER (1745-1822) is undoubtedly the most celebrated of all the smugglers associated with Bournemouth and the surrounding heath. He was born in Wiltshire, but his smuggling career probably dates to his marriage aged 23 to an innkeeper's daughter from Thorney Down, on the edge of Cranborne Chase. Soon he was landing contraband on the then desolate beaches between Poole and Christchurch, some of which undoubtedly ended up in the cellars of Howe Lodge, his house in Kinson (demolished in 1958).

As his reputation grew, so did his smuggling band. His gang numbered about 50, all dressed in a specially designed livery of powdered hair and white smocks, hence their name – the 'White Wigs'. He was especially keen on smuggling wine, brandy, silk and tea – very expensive in those days with a high rate of tax.

Gulliver boasted that neither he nor his men had ever killed anybody in pursuit of their activities and, in 1782, he applied for the pardon that had then been offered by the government. It seems he then limited his activities to only wine, and legend has it that he warned George III of a French plot to assassinate him. This probably explains why his men, once seen on a two mile long convoy carrying smuggled goods, were not arrested. There is no factual evidence, only a story, that the King said, '*Let Gulliver smuggle as much as he likes*'.

Bribery obviously kept informants, the Excise and military from turning him in, although on one occasion one of his band was taken to a Christchurch doctor for the removal of a gunshot wound. The youthful Earl of Malmesbury saw kegs of brandy being hidden on his father's land and he was bribed with a barrel to say nothing. In 1780, the Earl of Shaftesbury on a visit to Hurn Court saw a line of smugglers with contraband riding past his host's window. No one said a word, not even to the detachment of the Royal Horse Artillery from Christchurch Barracks who came out to track them down. In later life Gulliver began a legitimate retail wine business, using the stock he had squirrelled away in his many hiding places.

There are stories that underground tunnels used by smugglers exist around St. Andrew's Church, Kinson, and others towards Butcher's Coppice, but these are romantic rumours. An old, retired Water Company worker who had to dig for a living all over the area said, '*If any tunnels large enough for men to walk along were there, I would have found them. I found spaces and some idiots got excited and said they were used by smugglers. But they were never more than a foot round and used for drainage*'.

Even a large tomb in St. Andrew's churchyard was said to store contraband but no evidence of this has yet been found.

Isaac Gulliver eventually attained respectability: his daughter married a banker from Wimborne whose descendant was Lieut. General Sir John Fryer. Gulliver died at the age of 77 in 1822, and a stone slab in the central aisle of Wimborne Minster marks his burial place.

But smuggling was not always a gentleman's pastime. Richard Trotman

Informing on Smugglers

Smugglers like Isaac Gulliver did not take kindly to being informed upon and retribution invariably followed. A favourite way to treat an informer was to abduct him and then take him to France or to the Channel Islands where he would be left to find his own way home. The *Salisbury and Winchester Journal* reported such a case in 1726. A group of eight smugglers, pretending to be a press gang, laid hands on Joseph Manual at his home at Iford and took him across the heath to Decoy Pond House in Bourne Chine – approximately where the War Memorial is now situated. Here Joseph was held until a boat was leaving for Alderney on a smuggling trip. He was left at Alderney to get home as best he could.

was '*barbarously murdered on the shore near Poole, the 24th March, 1795*' and was buried in St. Andrew's Church, Kinson. On his tombstone is written:

A little tea, one leaf I did not steal,
For guiltless blood shed I to God appeal;
Put tea in one scale, human blood in t'other,
And think what 'tis to slay a harmless brother.

Radclyffe HALL (1886-1943) was born in Durley Road. She was a poet and a prize-winning novelist. Her book *The Well of Loneliness* (1928) dealt with lesbianism and was not published in this country for many years.

Tony HANCOCK (d. 1968). Durlston Court Hotel, Gervis Road, was the childhood home of this famous comedian. The family moved there from the Railway Hotel, Holdenhurst Road. His first engagement was entertaining the troops at the Sacred Heart Church on Richmond Hill. A plaque may be seen outside the Durlston Hotel.

Neville HEATH (1917-46) was the sadistic murderer of Doreen Marshall whose body was found in Branksome Dene Chine in 1946 when both were on holiday in the Town. He is one of the most infamous murderers of all time.

Amanda HOLDEN, actress, was born in Bournemouth.

Sir Henry IRVING (1838-1905), the famous actor, often visited Bournemouth, not only to play at the local theatres of the time, but to play in charity performances with his friend Shelley at Boscombe Manor. He stayed at the Royal Bath Hotel and there is an Irving Room in the Russell-Cotes Museum.

J.D. JONES OM, (Revd.) was the renowned Minister of Richmond Hill Congregational Church for 39 years. In addition to receiving the Order of Merit, he was made a Freeman of the Borough of Bournemouth in March 1938.

John KEBLE (1792-1866) came here for the sake of his wife's health to Brookside, now part of the Hermitage Hotel where there is a suite named after him. Simplistically put, he founded the Anglo Catholic tradition of the Church of England. He worshipped daily at St. Peter's Church where the Lady Chapel is called the Keble Chapel. Keble College, Oxford, was built as his memorial.

Dr. Horace Maybray KING, came as Head of English with his evacuated school in the Second World War from Southampton to Bournemouth School, and played a large part in the Hampshire Spitfire Fund. After the war he entered Parliament and became Speaker of the House of Commons in 1965.

Lillie LANGTRY (1853-1929) was the actress daughter of the Dean of Jersey. She was mistress to King Edward VII who built a house (now a hotel) for her in the town.

D.H. LAWRENCE (1885-1930) spent one month in a boarding house in St. Peter's Road where he revised his story *The Traveller*. He is best known for *Women in Love* and *Lady Chatterley's Lover*.

Ethel LE NEVE owned a tea room/café for about 40 years at Iford. She

was the mistress of Dr. Crippen and, disguised as a boy, she went with him
to the United States where they were arrested for murder as they
disembarked from a liner. They were the first to be arrested by means of
wireless telegraphy. He was hanged in 1910; she was found not guilty.

Julian MACLAREN-ROSS wrote *The Weeping and the Laughter*
(1953) based on his childhood memories of Southbourne.

Guglielmo MARCONI (1874-1937) had a broadcasting station at the
Court Royal (then the Madeira Hotel) by the BIC from which he sent
wireless signals across the Atlantic in 1901. He was awarded the Nobel
Prize.

MANTOVANI, the well-known band leader, was buried in the Central
Cemetery in 1980.

Freddie MILLS (1919-65) the World Light Heavy Weight boxer, was
born in Terrace Road. There was a memorial to him in the Pleasure
Gardens but as it was often vandalised, it was shifted to the Littledown
Leisure Centre.

Melita NORWOOD (1912-2005) was born in Bournemouth. As a spy
for the Soviet Union, she passed secret documents concerning nuclear
weapons to her KGB handlers.

Sir Hubert PARRY (1848-1918) was born in Bournemouth on
Richmond Hill where is mounted a blue plaque. He was one of the first to
be baptised at St. Peter's Church. He became a famous composer,
especially of church music and of *Jerusalem* and *The Londonderry Air*. He
was Director of the Royal College of Music.

William PIKE, born in Moordown in 1591, converted to Roman
Catholicism, and was put to death as a traitor at Dorchester. He was
beatified by Pope Pius in 1923.

Dilys POWELL, educated at Talbot Heath School, became a famous
film critic.

Francis RATTENBURY, a British-born architect famous in Canada,
retired to Bournemouth to live in Manor Road where he was murdered in
1935. The case was a *cause célèbre* of the time (see the next chapter).

Henry REEVE, editor of *The Edinburgh Review* lived here in his
retirement.

Thomas ROHAN wrote the revealing *Confessions of a Dealer*.

C.S. ROLLS, of motor car and flying fame, was killed at an air display in 1910 where St. Peter's School playing fields are now situated. A Memorial has been built there.

Michael ROBERTS, a pupil of Bournemouth School, is known for his *Critique of Poetry*.

Merton (1836) and Annie RUSSELL-COTES bought the Bath Hotel in 1876 and in it exhibited his art collection. He built East Cliff Hall as his home and, on Annie's death, it became the Russell-Cotes Museum with their possessions furnishing it (see page 80).

Elisabeth SCOTT was born in 1898 in Poole Road. She became an architect with Jackson, Greenham and Down and won the open competition with her design of the Stratford-on-Avon Memorial Theatre.

Mary Woolstonecraft SHELLEY (1797-1851) was married to the famous poet, Percy Byshe Shelley. In her own right she was famous as the writer of *Frankenstein* (1818). She is buried in St. Peter's churchyard.

Ann SIDNEY from Parkstone won Miss World in 1985 and made her first stage appearance in the summer season production of *Lock Up Your Daughters* at the Palace Court Theatre in Westover Road.

F.E. SMITH has lived in Bournemouth for many years. He is a prolific novelist and his most famous book, *633 Squadron*, was made into a successful film.

Robert Louis STEVENSON (1850-1904) lived at Skerryvore in Westbourne where he wrote *Kidnapped* and *Dr. Jekyll and Mr. Hyde* between 1884 and 1887. A road has been named after him.

John Barnett SMITH lived here 1889-1909. He was author of *The History of the English Parliament*.

Andy SUMMERS, who attended Summerbee Secondary School, became a member of the popular 1980s pop group 'Police'.

Sir Henry TAYLOR (1800-86) author, playwright and poet lived in Hinton Road and was buried in St. Peter's Churchyard.

Vladimir TCHERTKOV led a group of Russian exiles to England. In 1898 he bought The Old Water Tower, Iford Lane, where he set up a printing works to publish books in Russian which had been banned in his native country. He arranged for them to be smuggled back there. He also bought Tuckton House to store Tolstoy's manuscripts which were sent to

The memorial plaque to The Hon. C.S. Rolls killed at this spot at the Centenary Air Display in 1910. It is in the playing fields of St Peter's School, Southbourne.

Robert Louis Stevenson

The famous author lived for two of his three years in Bournemouth, 1885-87, in a large house at the end of Middle Road named 'Skerryvore'. Here he wrote *Kidnapped* and *Dr Jekyll and Mr Hyde*. It was badly damaged by a land mine in November 1940 and had to be demolished. The site was bought for a rest garden, the footings of the house were laid out in stone, and a small, stone lighthouse about four feet high with a glass dome was erected. This was a copy of the Skerryvore lighthouse off the coast of Argyll built by Stevenson's uncle.

On the bridge at Alum Chine is a plaque commemorating his stay in Bournemouth where he '*lived like a weevil in a biscuit*'. (RLS's words.) Robert Louis Stevenson Avenue is named after him.

Dr. Bodley Scott

Dr. Bodley Scott was a gifted and highly qualified general practitioner in Bournemouth. He longed for a prestigious appointment at St. Bartholomew's Hospital in London. One evening, a telephone call came to him to take up an appointment at Bart's provided he could start the next morning at 9 o'clock. The doctors in his practice allowed him to leave immediately. Later, Bodley Scott was appointed to be Physician to HM Queen Victoria. His father was physician to R.L. Stevenson when the author lived in Bournemouth.

In the mid 1930s, crowds of people would watch J. Suchomlim, the artist in sand sculpture at work near Bournemouth Pier. His work was rarely vandalised, though occasionally the wind and the sea attacked it. The third notice in the background reads: "Only sand, water and colour used". But many swore there was another, secret ingredient.

him by their author for safe keeping. They are now on exhibition in the Tolstoy Museum in Moscow. Chertkov's mother owned 'Slavanka' in Belle Vue Road.

George THOMAS, Speaker of the House of Commons, was a frequent visitor here and he spoke at various local churches.

Flora THOMPSON, author of *Lark Rise to Candleford*, lived here for a time.

Dame Sybil THORNDYKE and her husband Sir Lewis Casson, both famous actors, lived for a time at Kinson House (now no more) along the Wimborne Road. She created the title role of *Saint Joan* in Bernard Shaw's famous play. Russell Thorndyke, her brother, lived there for a time and it is thought he was inspired by the stories of smuggling in the area to write his Dr. Syn novels.

J.R.R. TOLKEIN (1892-1973) stayed often and for long periods at the Hotel Miramar on the East Cliff from the 1950s until 1972, as indicated by the blue plaque on the south wall. He was the author of *The Hobbit* and *The Lord of the Rings*, successful as novels and in screen adaptations. He is probably the most prestigious writer connected with the town. He died in a Bournemouth nursing home.

Mike TOMLINSON, a former Bournemouth School pupil, became Chief Inspector of Schools, and in 2003, he was appointed Chairman of a Government Working Group studying education for 14-19 year olds.

Paul VERLAINE (1844-96), French poet, came to teach here at a private school in Surrey Road for about a year after he had been imprisoned in France for wounding his young male lover, Rimbaud, who was also a poet. Surprisingly, a blue plaque to him has been erected.

Virginia WADE, daughter of a Vicar of Holy Trinity Church, lived here for a few years. She was Ladies' Singles Champion at Wimbledon in 1977, and is a regular TV tennis commentator.

Beatrice (Potter) WEBB (1858-1943) attended a school which was on the site of the petrol station at the top of Bath Hill. She lived with her father at the Kildare Hotel, Bath Hill, and then married Sydney Webb.

They were famous early socialists, trade unionists and also founders of the Fabian Society and of the London School of Economics.

(Sir) Roy WELENSKY, buried in the Jewish Cemetery at Kinson in 1991, was a Prime Minister of Southern Rhodesia before it became Zimbabwe. He had retired to Blandford.

Percy WHITLOCK, a nationally renowned recitalist and composer, was organist at St. Stephen's Church from 1930-5 and Borough Organist at the Pavilion Theatre, 1932-46, where a plaque outside the entrance was placed in his memory in 2004.

P.C. WREN (1885-1941) lived in Talbot Woods. He was author of novels, the most popular of which was *Beau Geste*.

Past Mayors

1890-2005

There have been 93 different Mayors of Bournemouth from 1890 to 2005, a period of 114 years, and photographs of each of them wearing the Robes of Office hang in a corridor at the left of Reception in the Town Hall.

Nine of them were Mayors for three years and their portraits hang in the Mayor's Parlour. They were: J.E. Beale (1902-05); Bridge (07-10); McColmont Hill (11-14); Cartwright (20-23); Thwaites (25-28); Bright (29-32); and J.W. Moore (46-49). Four Mayors held office for two consecutive years: Parsons (05-07); Robson (15-17); Bishop (17-19) and Mate (23-25).

1890-1900

Hankinson and Rebbeck, the first two Mayors, were both estate agents and Rebbeck liked to be called 'Colonel' as he held that rank in the 4th Hants TA. Newlyn brought Dan Godfrey to the town. Hirons kept himself in the background. Russell-Cotes gave the town its Museum, and was not a Councillor when he was asked to be Mayor, still a unique honour. Hosker was the youngest Mayor in the country at 39 and was later knighted for his services to the Conservative Party. Hoare was a stonemason; nothing more is known about him. Webber went to school with Thomas Hardy. Lawson appeared to be the only non-Conservative Mayor for many years as he was Treasurer of the local Liberal Association; he was Secretary of the East Cliff Congregational (UR) Church for 57 years.

1901-1923

Frost was defeated at an election after only six years' service as a councillor. J.E. Beale led the fight for the Undercliff Drive and for the Pavilion; he started the department store which bears his name. Parsons died in office as Deputy Mayor at the age of 47. Bridge became Mayor after only one year's service on the Council; the shop which bears his name is still at Horseshoe Common. Hunt was born at Holdenhurst and became a builder. McColmont Hill was returned unopposed at every election. Druitt had been a Clerk to the Commissioners and a Town Clerk

Cartwright

(Cllr Sir Charles Cartwright was Chairman of the Finance Committee at the age of 93.)

'I find that I attended six of the Mayors medically, including Cartwright at the end of his life. Templeman approached me to see if I could get him to resign from the Council. I remember the priest coming out of the house and saying as he met me. "I fear Sir Charles is sinking." I cured his lobar pneumonia with Penicillin injections.'
Dr James Fisher

The drawing is one of a series from *The Bournemouth Times* 'Who's What', by the artist John Garling of people connected with Bournemouth.

A Civic Luncheon

The Civic Luncheon in 1913 was held in the Municipal College. The local press published the names of the 126 people who had accepted invitations and 28 who had been unable to attend. Only two ladies were present and they were members of the Distress Committee. Speeches were reported, some in full. In today's *Echo*, they would fill at least eight pages, probably more as there were 27 speeches.

The first toast was to the Clergy and Ministers of all Denominations, and there were three responses: from a representative of the Church of England, from the Roman Catholic Church, and from the Free Churches.

Sir Daniel Morris proposed the toast of the County Borough of Bournemouth to which the Mayor responded.

A toast was made to the returning Aldermen by Councillor Duka, and responses were made by Aldermen Beale, Youngman, Druitt, Mate and Robson.

The Deputy Mayor welcomed new Councillors and thanked former members for their service. Cllr. Panchen thanked the Deputy Mayor, and the nine new councillors responded! Cllr. Godfrey proposed the Toast of the Officers of the Corporation, and the Town Clerk (Mr. Ashling) responded with a humorous speech which was reported almost in full. Cllr. Evans proposed the last Toast: to the Press. Mr. E.A. Colborne responded. No mention is made of what he said, such was the modesty of the press in those days.

of the new Borough. Robson held a position in Bournemouth's Volunteer Fire Brigade for 30 years and was with Baden Powell on Brownsea Island when the Boy Scouts were formed. Bishop, a jeweller, issued the Bournemouth Peace Medal in 1919 for all local school children. Cartwright, knighted in 1939, was Chairman of Finance at the age of 93.

1923-1940

Bodley Scott died while holding the office of Mayor, after having been on the Council for only two years. Mate's name was given to the clock with no figures on the Tower at the Lansdowne as Mate's Folly. Thwaites was a President of Bournemouth's Chamber of Trade. Bright owned one of the local departmental stores and he had a vast collection of butterflies and moths; he was killed in a road accident. Edgecombe, born in Devon, was a wholesale grocer. Harris traded in tobacco, cotton and rum on the West Coast of Africa and was known as 'John Blunt'. Rebbeck, son of an earlier Mayor, was CO of Bournemouth's Home Guard. J.B.C. Beale, also the son of a former Mayor, produced a small history of Bournemouth for every local school child. Dickinson was always returned unopposed to the Council in the West Cliff Ward; he owned a Joinery Company. Hayward, a Chairman of AFC Bournemouth, gave an annual tea party for the poor in his area.

1940-1950

Little, nicknamed 'The Dictator', was Controller of the local ARP and for 30 years was returned unopposed at the Council elections. Empson was the first Labour Councillor to be Mayor; he was President of the Local Co-

Operative Society. Summerbee never missed a meeting of the Education Committee of which he was a member for 41 years; Summerbee Schools were named after him, but they are now The Bishop of Winchester C of E Comprehensive School and the Queen's Park Junior School. Richards, a lawyer, worked for the 'Pru'. H.C. Brown, a hotelier, died of a heart attack whilst driving along Tregonwell Road to attend a Council meeting. Old founded the gentlemen's outfitters in Westover Road still carried on by his family. J.W. Moore was the MD of Wilkins, the Bakers, and his son was a Captain of Hampshire CCC. J.H. Turner was a retired Lieutenant Commander in the RN and liked to be called by his rank.

1950-1960

Thompson, one of the few Mayors to have been born in Bournemouth, was a qualified soccer referee. McInnes, a Knight of St Gregory, owned the Norfolk Hotel and was killed in a car accident. Benwell MC was awarded the BEM for setting up the local Auxiliary Fire Service. Mears, who was chairman of six committees all at the same time, gained the OBE for being Controller of ARP wardens and the Civil Defence during World War Two. Smith, who owned a fabric shop in the town, had served at Gallipoli and was a President of the Meyrick Park Golf Club. Willoughby, a supporter of the arts, was the first Mayor to have been born in this century. Templeman, CBE, born in the town, was Chairman of the Finance Committee, of the Social Services Committee and of the Wessex Hospital Trust. Whitelock was the MD of the Shamrock and Rambler Coaches which his father had founded in 1880. Henry Brown, hotelier, was a Chairman of the Education Committee. Barney, gassed during World War One, was a tailor.

1960-1970

Mrs. Bicknell, OBE, the first woman Mayor, was a very strong Conservative and Chairman of Education. Deric Scott, an undertaker, also became the first Chairman of Dorset County Council in 1974, and a Deputy Lieutenant and High Sheriff of the county. Adams founded his own model car company and was a top-class ballroom dancer. Morris from Coventry worked in a solicitors' office. Whitelegg, an estate agent, welcomed to Bournemouth HM The Queen and the Duke of Edinburgh; he retired as a Councillor after 50 years' service in 2002, having been made a Freeman and an Honorary Alderman of the Borough. Purdy, a greengrocer, was a keen fisherman. Green, OBE, a licensee, was the first Chairman of the new Dorset County Council Policy & Resources Committee; he was also Chairman of the Southern Tourist Board. Beckett, an estate agent, became known as 'Mr. Safety' as he chaired the Road Safety Committee for so long.

1970-1980

Lane, a hotelier, was Vice Chairman of AFC Bournemouth. Judd became President of the Bournemouth Londoners' Club, and was a builder. Miss Swetenham was a Factory Inspector who, on Planning matters, always sought to preserve trees. Dillon, always referred to as 'Major', was not able to serve his full term as Mayor when Bournemouth lost its County status. Forman, owner of a garage on the site of the BIC, served for only part of a year owing to the abolition of Bournemouth as a County Borough; he was made a Freeman of the Borough. R. Turner, who worked for Bowmakers, was surprisingly defeated at an election. Masters, a driving instructor, was Chairman of Amenities for both Bournemouth and Dorset Councils. Patton worked in his father-in-law's textile factory and was Deputy Mayor for two years. Jaffe was unable to serve as Deputy Mayor owing to the demands of his medical practice. Frank Beale's grandfather and father were previous Mayors, and three of his uncles had been Councillors; after he did not stand for re-election in 1987, it was the first time since 1900 there had been no Beale from the Department store on the Council. Kellaway, a Bournemouthian and an estate agent, also served on Dorset County Council.

1980-1990

Day, a former headmaster, also served on Dorset County Council and on the Western Orchestral Society Board. Anstee, a Londoner, was a hotelier, a keen philatelist and a top Freemason. Mrs. Sheila McQueen became the first lady Honorary Alderman, the office of Alderman having been discontinued in 1974; she was also a Dorset County Councillor and a Governor of five different schools. Mrs. Jeanne Curtis, whose father had laid many of the town's Victorian drains, was a marketing consultant in the carpet industry; she was also a Dorset County Councillor. Filer, a chartered accountant, first joined the Council in 1969, retired, and was re-elected, together with his wife in 1999. Wootton, an estate agent, was Vice Chairman of the Dorset Police Authority for seven years; he instituted the past Mayors' Annual Dinner. Crone, a retired headmaster, was on the Board of the Western Orchestral Society and a member of the Wessex Sports Council. Mrs. Barbara Siberry, who read children's stories for the BBC, welcomed Princess Diana, The Princess Royal and Princess Margaret to the Town. Mrs. Jacky Harris, MBE, was a Board Member of the National Chamber of Trade and of the Bournemouth International Festival. Bostock, an estate agent and developer, was a county tennis player.

1990-2005

Coe, a County Youth Club Leader, was Mayor during the 100th Anniversary of the Town's Borough Status. Bennett, the second Labour Mayor, son of a previous Councillor, was on Dorset County Council for nearly 20 years, and was posthumously made an Honorary Alderman of the Town. Mrs. Margaret Hogarth, a former Conservative, stood as an Independent Conservative Candidate for Parliament; she later joined the Liberal Democrats. Whittaker, an ambulanceman, was a Labour Councillor until he was expelled over policy matters. Millward, a GP with an interest in alternative medicine, became Liberal Democrat Leader of the Council. Mrs. Pamela Harris, a former professional actress, ran a hotel for 20 years, and collected the European Entente Florale for the Town. Mrs. Jean Moore was the first Liberal Democrat woman Councillor to represent the Borough on Dorset County Council. Brushett worked in the poultry industry and represented Wallisdown on Dorset County Council and on Bournemouth. Rawlings, a former Member of General Synod, was Chairman of the Bournemouth Little Theatre Club; he became an Honorary Alderman in 2003. Courtney was a Divisional Officer in Dorset Fire Brigade and he serves on the Combined Fire Authority. Grower, a Chartered Accountant, was leader of the Labour Group and stood as a parliamentary candidate. Eyre, also a Chartered Accountant, was a Leader of the Liberal Democrats on the Council and his main hobby is the theatre; he became an Honorary Alderman in 2003. Baldwin, an expert on ultra-violet data recorders, was a local hotelier for 20 years. Mrs Anne Rey, a social worker and leader of the Independent Group is daughter of Whitelegg, a previous Mayor. Mrs Emily Morrell-Cross runs her own home for the mentally ill and still proudly retains her accent from her birthplace in Ashton-under-Lyme. Taylor, locally born, was a detached youth worker; he serves on many organisations in West Howe.

Twenty-eight mayors have been locally born and a surprisingly high number have hailed from London. Of those Mayors now deceased, all but two were buried or cremated in Bournemouth. McColmont was buried in Paignton and Frost in Langton Matravers.

Only one Mayor died in office: T.B. Scott, which explains why Cartwright, his Deputy, had an extra 'year' as Mayor. Benwell became very ill while in office so Mears, his Deputy, assumed office for the remainder of the year.

The first woman Mayor was Alderman Mrs. Bessie Bicknell (1961-62) who joined the Council in 1953 to sit with three other women Councillors. Her portrait hangs in the Mayor's Parlour. The first woman Councillor was Mrs. Florence Laney, who had to serve from 1919 until 1935 before she was joined by another woman. By the end of the 20th Century, 17 women have been Mayor, and they are addressed as 'Mr. Mayor', much to the delight and merriment of many.

The Arms of Bournemouth

The arms date from 1891 and at the top is a Pine Tree (not a Palm Tree, for the town was once known as 'Pine City'). It grows from a mountain on which are four English Roses mounted on a Helmet. This is on a shield quarterly or (gold) and azure (blue) with a cross fleurie counter charged. On the first and fourth quarters is a Lion Rampant holding the Hampshire Rose in its paws (the town was once in that county). In the second quarter are six marlets (sand martins nest in cliffs); in the third are four salmon (representing the fish in the River Stour).

The motto is *Pulchritudo et Salubritas* meaning 'Beauty and Health'.

Mrs Alma Rattenbury who wrote, published and broadcast music under the name of Rozanne, was found not guilty of the murder of her husband.

Paleness Explained

At the Old Bailey, Stoner's paleness was commented upon by one of the counsel who suggested that frequency of sexual intercourse in one so young could cause this paleness which all in court could see! Even Stoner's defence added to the love affair in a grandiloquent manner.

'*This crime is, in my submission, almost inexplicable in a young Englishman. You might expect it in a man of hot blood and of Latin race, urged on by jealousy or some kindred emotion, but is it the sort of thing one expects in a lad of 17 or 18, and an English lad?*'

THIRTEEN

Two Murders & Several Ghosts

The Rattenbury Murder

Two notorious murders which are nationally remembered happened in Bournemouth. The Rattenbury murder was a *cause célèbre*, inspiring books and a play by Terence Rattigan called *Cause Célèbre* which has been performed in the West End and on television. It was an unbelievable story of love and death, almost on a par with Romeo and Juliet; and 3,000 people, mostly women, attended the funeral of Alma Rattenbury at Wimborne Road Cemetery on 8 June 1935. Yet her gravestone remains unmarked.

Francis Rattenbury, aged 68, and his wife Alma, 33 years younger, had advertised in the *Echo* in September 1934, for a '*Daily willing lad, 14-18 for housework. Scout trained preferred. Apply 5 Manor Road*'. George Stoner, aged 17, was appointed, and a month later he drove Mrs. Rattenbury and her housekeeper/companion, Irene Riggs, for a few days' break at a hotel in Oxford. Here, Stoner was seduced by his employer. She possibly remembered her wealthy husband, now becoming an alcoholic, telling her, '*Lead your life as if I had already gone*'.

They all lived together in Villa Madeira, the Rattenburys' home, where despite their age difference Alma and George Stoner fell in love. When George discovered that the Rattenburys were to spend the night in Bridport on business and therefore might have to sleep together, he became jealous. Later that night, dressed in his pyjamas, George got into bed with Alma and admitted that he had hurt 'Ratz' (Mr. Rattenbury's nickname.) The injured man was taken to a Nursing Home in Owls Road. Mrs. Rattenbury was arrested and charged with wounding and causing grievous bodily harm with intent to murder.

Four days later, Francis Rattenbury died, so the case became one of murder. Shortly after, George Stoner was jointly charged with murder. At the committal proceedings even the prosecution had no idea which of the two was telling the truth. In prison, Alma Rattenbury insisted she was guilty. Stoner admitted that he had hit Rattenbury. This was unusual in murder cases where two were charged; one usually tried to shift the guilt on to the other. But not in this case.

At the end of the trial Alma Rattenbury was found Not Guilty. Stoner was found Guilty. The road outside the Central Criminal Courts was crowded with thousands of people, nearly all of whom were on the youth's side. A few days later, Alma Rattenbury returned to Bournemouth by train, alighted at Christchurch and walked to the river by The Lakes, where she

138

stabbed herself to death. She could not live without Stoner.

Three weeks later, Stoner was reprieved from being hanged. He served seven years in prison, then joined the army for War Service. He married in the 1960s and lived for the rest of his life in Bournemouth until he died when he was in his eighties.

Neville Heath

Neville Heath's name would appear in the top five of the most well-known murderers of the twentieth century. Indeed, just after the Second World War, his name attracted tens of thousands to Bournemouth as tourists, just as the Rattenbury murder had a decade earlier.

Heath was first charged with the murder of Mrs. Margery Gardiner, a 32-year-old masochist, whose body had been found in an hotel in London in 1946. The second of the two murders was committed in Bournemouth.

Neville Heath, sadistic murderer.

He had booked into the Tollard Royal Hotel, now flats a short distance behind the Bournemouth International Centre, as Group Captain Rupert Brooke. He had no luggage, but he wore the Hawkes Club tie given to those who had won a double blue at Cambridge. All who remembered him spoke of '*his good appearance, good physique, wavy, fair hair*'.

Doreen Marshall, aged 21, daughter of a respectable director of a well known departmental store in London, was staying at the Norfolk Hotel on Richmond Hill, using some of her gratuity from the Women's Royal Naval Service to pay for her holiday. She first met Heath whilst walking with another girl on the West Promenade. She had dinner with him at his hotel and, just after midnight, he said he would walk her back to her hotel. That was the last anyone saw of Doreen Marshall alive.

After her disappearance was reported in the press, Heath telephoned the police to enquire if they had a photograph of the missing woman, and two hours later he went to the police station to see it. This over-confidence was his downfall. The policeman on duty had seen Heath's photograph on the front page of *The Police Gazette*, and when he asked, '*Is that you*?' the unflappable Heath answered, '*Good Lord, no! But I agree it is like me*'. It was becoming cool, so he asked that his jacket be fetched from his hotel. This was either a thoughtless piece of bravado or a way of signalling his guilt. The police found in a pocket a first class ticket from Waterloo to Bournemouth, the one that had been issued to Doreen Marshall; and a Bournemouth West Station ticket for a left-luggage locker, which contained in a suitcase a blood-stained scarf and a riding whip which had been used by Heath during the course of the murder.

The police took Heath to London where, after identification, he was charged with the London murder of Margery Gardiner. Meanwhile, the body of Miss Marshall had been found naked under a rhododendron bush at Branksome Dene Chine. The crowds intent on seeing the body were held at bay by the police with the greatest difficulty. The *Echo* reported that a '*great crowd of holiday makers*' followed the corpse as it was taken to Poole mortuary.

The trial of Heath, the handsome sadist, began at The Old Bailey in

This seat built into the wall of a property in Seafield Road/Iford Lane marks the spot where the body of Irene Wilkins was found. Thomas Allaway, a chauffeur, was hanged for her murder in 1921. Many believed he was innocent.

September 1946 for the murder of Margery Gardiner. He was later charged with the murder of Doreen Marshall as well, but never faced trial. He was found guilty of the murder of Margery Gardiner, and in the condemned cell before his execution he wrote:

'To my mind this is just another one-way operation, but if there is anything in this reincarnation business, please break your morning egg very gently for the next couple of months, because it may be me.'

He was hanged on 26 October 1946 at Pentonville Prison. The *Bournemouth Echo* reported the scene outside the prison when the notice certifying the execution was displayed: *There was a melee and fighting and pushing, and police had to restore order.*

The Ghosts of Bournemouth

The Opera House, Boscombe
People who patronise the building have been warned. A stone devil is on the building opposite to warn those who enter the Opera House, and this has been there ever since the theatre was opened. A former manager reported that he stayed behind after work one Monday night talking with a few members of staff in the main hall when all the lights went on. An alarm sounded and he went to investigate, only to discover that the back fire escape was wide open. *'The next day when we looked at the security camera tapes,'* he said, *'a figure could be seen moving towards the console before the lights went on'*.

A clown who hanged himself under the stage has been seen, and five more ghosts are rumoured to haunt the building. But this hasn't stopped the thousands who visit the nightclub there every week.

– *Bournemouth University Students' Union Nerve Magazine*

The Shelley Room
When the building was being used as an Art College, a British Telecom engineer was repairing the phones upstairs. He asked if there was a presence in the room as he could feel something which he couldn't explain. He found it rather off-putting. The person he spoke to was a medium and he agreed there was something mysterious about that room. He had experienced a 'feeling' there, too, but he was sure she was a peaceful spirit.

Phantom Lillie
There have been reports that Lillie Langtry, mistress of the Prince of Wales, later King Edward VII, and known in London society as 'Jersey Lily', haunts her old house in Derby Road – now the attractive Langtry Manor Hotel.

Her presence is particularly felt, we are told, around 4 p.m. in the kitchen. There have even been instances of her ghostly carriage drawing up the driveway of the house next door in the early hours of the morning. The Prince has been seen in a downstairs room of the hotel.

Chine Court Hotel
This hotel in Boscombe Spa Road had a large hook in the ceiling over the rear staircase where a man once hanged himself. It is claimed that in one of the bedrooms, although the bed is continually being made up, there always appears the indentation of a body.

This, of course, is news to the owners of the hotel who have owned it for 50 years.

The Town Hall
There are two ghosts in this building which was used as a military hospital during the First World War. A wounded Gurkha soldier is said to walk the basement corridors: he also made frequent appearances when dances were held in the now demolished Grand Hall.

A man committed suicide by throwing himself from the fourth floor. His misty figure can occasionally be seen pacing its corridor.

Holdenhurst Road Fire Station

The building is now a student pub called the Old Fire Station, but the top floor is haunted by the dead bodies supposedly stored there after the May 1943 air raid which killed over 50 servicemen and women staying in the Metropole Hotel at the Lansdowne. During a night watch, two firemen sleeping in the Station Officer's bedroom were woken by smoke blowing through the door. Thinking it was the other firemen, they told them to stop messing around. But the smoke suddenly shot into the room and started swirling in circles above the bed. Almost immediately, the bed started to shake violently, and the firemen decided that now would be a good time to leave.

The Legend of Butcher's Coppice

It is well known that several tunnels exist between Alum Chine, Branksome Chine and the Kinson area. One of these tunnels ends in Butcher's Coppice. Mr. Butcher, who originally owned the land, was a famous smuggler. One day, just as his band of smugglers reached the end of the tunnel at the Coppice, the Customs Officers arrived and the tunnel was hastily filled in – but, unfortunately, one of the smugglers was buried alive. The point at the end of the tunnel is just by the main water tap. Now, if you should need to get up in the night to go to the toilet block, go straight there and back again. Should you go near the tap, you may hear a scratching noise which is the ghost of the buried smuggler trying to escape.

Boscombe Manor

In 1852, a play called *The Wreck Ashore* was being acted on the Boscombe Manor (Shelley Theatre) stage, when a Norwegian sailor was brought up to the house in a state of insensibility, having been rescued from the barque *William Glen Anderson* which had been wrecked off the coast of Boscombe. He received every possible attention from his host and hostess, who did not relax their efforts on his behalf until he had fallen into a natural sleep. But the next morning, when they sent to enquire as to his condition, he had disappeared and no news was ever received of his fate. Servants of the time assert that his strangely opportune appearance had been but a myth.

From *Harbour to Harbour*, Nancy Bell.

Hinton Road

An old woman pushing a bicycle along the pavement at about eleven o'clock at night has been seen near the Wessex Christian Centre in Hinton Road. She smiles graciously and pedals away to vanish immediately. This sighting has been reported when the road is practically empty. It is thought this ghost has a connection with the building when it was known as the Palace Court Theatre.

Pug's Hole, Glenferness Avenue
A smuggler was killed here on this route for smuggled goods on their way to Wimborne. His ghost has been seen by people taking their dogs for walks.

Hengistbury Head
It is inevitable that a ghost should be reported to appear in this remote part of the town which was often used by smugglers. Those who report seeing him say he was carrying kegs of brandy.

Albert Road
Organ Lady appears in a long, grey dress in the balcony of what was once the Theatre Royal in Albert Road.

In the same road, in the *Echo* building, a ghostly mist appears in one of the offices. But the press informs us that it does not hang about for long.

Holdenhurst Road Fire Station
Some years ago, a fireman met his death whilst practising on the tower at the rear of the premises. His ghost appears at nights standing in one of the tower openings as if waiting to jump.

FOURTEEN

Epilogue

The Land Use and Transportation Survey begun in 1964 laid the basis for further development in this part of Dorset: for housing, for industrial development, and for the road network. There are certain obvious gaps. But in Bournemouth it is difficult to imagine life without the Wessex Way to Ringwood and the M3 to London; the dual carriageway of the Town Centre Bypass; and the raised roadway by the Bournemouth Pier.

Bournemouth, Poole and Christchurch also anticipated present day water authorities and completed the inland treatment of sewage at Holdenhurst which, until the late 1960s, was discharged into the sea.

It is a matter of record that one of the major failures of the plans of those years was the lack of progress for many years in the establishment of adequate conference facilities to match the number of hotel and guest house rooms on offer.

The Bournemouth International Centre

It was in January 1970, that the then Development Committee of the Council received a first report on the possible provision of a conference hall seating 4,500 to 5,000 delegates with appropriate accompanying exhibition space, catering and car parking. Initially, a development which would extend the existing Pavilion complex by building out over Bath Road on to the East Cliff had been considered; but it became apparent that only the demolition of the somewhat run-down area to the west of Exeter Road could provide an adequate site for what seemed to be the minimum need.

There was general acceptance that the project was both desirable and worthwhile and the Council agreed to invitations being sent out widely for submission projects.

By November 1970, six potential large-scale projects had been drawn up on lines which would enable the Council to provide a leasehold site for suitable development. Two schemes were selected for detailed examination: one submitted by a Leeds Consortium and the second by an international group headed by a local firm of architects and a well known UK building contractor. It was this scheme which was favoured by the Development Committee, for they were impressed by the size and scope of the plans and also by the calibre and status of the firms associated with the development. The centre was to include a 200-bedroom hotel.

The Bournemouth International Centre.

When in due course the announcement was made that it was the international group scheme that was favoured, the period leading up to a special meeting of the Council was marked by an organised campaign. This, led by a prominent Alderman, denigrated the consortium, describing it as a 'Bahamas Mafia' and opined that the project was entirely out of keeping with the character of Bournemouth. At the Council Meeting the decision was taken by a large majority that negotiations be terminated.

In the year that followed, a further outline plan for a Development by the Council was prepared and submitted in 1974 to a public enquiry. Once more there was strenuous opposition led by the Chamber of Trade, the Victorian Society and others, and the cause was lost yet again.

Ultimately, it was not until 1984 that a building on the site which had been awaiting development since the early 1970s was completed and the present Bournemouth International Centre was opened.

Many small conferences for under 200 people are held in suitable hotels, and there are many of them in the town; but when it comes to those requiring accommodation for 4,000 delegates, their exhibitions, their administrators and the press, only the BIC with the Pavilion are large enough. The Labour Party Conference, held here in 2003, attracted 18,000 visitors who were expected to boost the local economy by £12 million. The BIC caterers estimated that they served 60,000 cups of tea and coffee, 50,000 sandwiches and 25,000 slices of cake. No estimate for the number of pints of beer and measures of spirits have been made. The profits from

BIC Land
Four hotels stood on the site occupied by the BIC which opened in 1984. They were the Solent Cliffs, The Meyrick Cliffs, The Regent Palace and The Beechcliffe. All of them were originally villas built in the 1870s which had been converted to guest Houses. A garage, Scientific Motors, was also on the site.

The Leisure Pool at the BIC which in 2005 was filled in to provide permanent additional exhibition space. Previously, and on a few occasions, it was emptied and a temporary floor erected over it to provide exhibition space or room for the world's press at Conservative or Labour party conferences. Notice the view of the sea for those swimming.

this enables the outside caterers to pay the hundreds of thousands of pounds a year to the Council for the privilege of providing catering in the building.

In 2003, a heated debate took place in the local press when the Council suggested that the BIC Leisure Pool should be closed so it could be turned into more exhibition space for the large conferences. Since the pool had been built, nearly all the larger hotels had provided their own heated pools for the use of their patrons. It finally closed in 2005.

Night life and Night clubs

In the 1990s it was hinted to one of the authorities in the town that there were too few pubs. Some conference delegates preferred to go to a pub rather than drink in the 'solemnity of our hotel'. Bournemouth University had expanded to over 10,000 students and they wanted more drinking places. In a short time there seemed to be a proliferation of new pubs, much to the annoyance of many Bournemouth residents. (There are 54 public houses in the Town, whereas the much smaller Weymouth has only two fewer.) The club scene in the town became an attraction for many young people who would visit them and stay in the smaller guest houses over the weekend, to return on Sunday to the various parts of the country from which they had travelled. 'Clubbing' had now become an attraction for short-stay visitors just as the beach was for others. The local press constantly received letters of complaint about the crowds of young people who thronged the street at night time in the St. Peter's Road and Horseshoe Common areas. Even on mid-week nights, at past eleven o'clock, coatless young women in the coldest weather might be seen queuing for entry to town centre clubs. They were lightly clad so they did not have to deposit coats in a cloakroom.

The Bournemouth International Centre attracts some of the biggest names in entertainment for a one night performance: Take That, Barry Manilow, Oasis, Will Young, Simply Red, Bryan Adams, and Kylie Minogue to name but a few. Members of the audience come from all over the country for the show. A surprising number stay over-night before travelling back home and this adds to the hotel occupancy rates. Times have changed from the holiday patterns of 50 years ago, and Bournemouth has had to move with the times. Gone are the days when a family would stay for a fortnight. The average stay today is five days, and that is usually a second holiday, the main one being abroad.

The Waterfront

The Waterfront Complex on the site of the old Pier Approach Baths was built by private enterprise. It was hoped wet weather entertainment would be provided by the IMAX cinema. But almost before it was opened in 1999, there was such a wave of protest from the public about the building's design that no enterprise in it had a fair chance. The local press was bombarded with letters of protest. The building, it was asserted,

The more attractive 'sea side' of the locally hated IMAX building, properly called The Waterfront Centre. The local planners were probably seduced by its roof which, it was emphasised at the planning meeting, echoed the waves of the sea. (From a watercolour by B.W. Barnes.)

blocked the view of the Purbecks when motoring down Bath Hill. It was a modern architectural monstrosity from the north side. Protesters conveniently forgot that the former Baths (only a metre lower) and three hotels (the Lynwood, the Rothesay and the Kildare) used to occupy the space now used as a car park immediately above the IMAX, as the building is erroneously called. Before their demolition, there was only a very limited view of the Purbecks coming down Bath Hill.

It was almost certain that the largest party on the Council, then the Liberal Democrats, suffered political defeat by the Conservatives at the May 2000 elections over this one issue: the IMAX. The Liberal Democrat administration had granted planning permission for the building. Unfortunately, the bleakest side of the building is the view most people see; the view from the beach is pleasing, with the design of the roof taking up the shape of waves of the nearby sea.

The Winter Gardens Debate

The provision for the arts in Bournemouth was argued about with occasional letters to the local newspapers in the late 1990s. They became an avalanche when the Winter Gardens began to be phased out and its closure was forecast. The Bournemouth Symphony Orchestra had changed its headquarters to the new Poole Arts Centre, now the Lighthouse, and the number of concerts in Bournemouth became fewer. The former stars of the entertainment world were either dead, retired or confined their appearances to television. Those who still made live appearances spread their names over the few resorts that could boast an (ever decreasing) summer season. The big stars were from the pop world

A view of what are surely Bournemouth's greatest attractions, its stunning setting and glorious beach. The watercolour by Mary How shows the Land Train which operates along the Promenade,

who would demand enormous halls for one night and usually fill them. The Bournemouth International Centre's Windsor Hall was able to accommodate these, providing seating for 3,500 with well over 4,000 standing room for the groups' ecstatic fans. Rod Stewart was the last mega star to fill the venue at £65 a seat in 2004. The Pavilion attracted few top class lyric-theatre-type shows as the Council's policy was never to offer a subsidy or a first call. Even a top show with nationally known stars during a summer season in the early 1990s was unable to make a profit.

Then, 'Save the Winter Gardens' became the cry. It was emphasised that it has one of the finest acoustics for music of any hall in the country, and it was remembered with fondness by generations of children who sang in the Annual Schools' Carol Festival there. But the live entertainment scene had changed over the years. The Bournemouth Orchestras were happily playing at the Lighthouse in Poole, which had not existed in the hey-day of the Winter Gardens. Nevertheless, The Friends gathered over 20,000 signatures for a petition to support their plea, and they received massive support from the local press. At the local elections in May 2003, the Liberal Democrats, who supported the petitioners, decimated the

The Winter Gardens.

This photography by Grahame Austin shows the beach, its groynes and the Esplanade stretching west to Alum Chine and Sandbanks.

Conservatives who were in favour of its demolition, to become the party in overall control at the Town Hall. For the second time in four years a building had probably led to the political change of leadership on the Bournemouth Council.

A firm of professional consultants was called in to report. Seven thousand questionnaires were sent out to interested parties, and members of the Citizens' Panel were interviewed. In March 2004 the report was made to Councillors, and a main supporter of the Winter Gardens said, *'Keeping it is not as straightforward as I thought it would be'*. And the professional consultant said, *'If the Winter Gardens were not here I wouldn't be recommending it'*. In any case, the Winter Gardens would require a yearly subsidy of between £250,000 and £2 million from the Council taxpayers – whichever of the options put forward was accepted by the Council. By mid 2005, the Friends of the Winter Gardens reported that they were unable to produce the £6 million they hoped to raise from private sources. However, if the Winter Gardens were sold to a developer, razed to the ground and replaced by flats, it would bring in a capital sum of about £10 million for the Council to spend on the Pavilion. Within about a year, minds on the Council began to change over the wisdom of keeping the Winter Gardens when it was announced in mid 2004 that the town's security system of CCTV cameras, which were amongst the first in the country and were past their sell-by date, would cost over £4 million to up-date. A large capital sum was needed. The town still waits for any plan to be finalised.

At the same time, two firms were regarded as suitable for developing the Terrace Mount car park for flats to produce the £6+ million which could be used to pay for alterations to the Winter Gardens. Opponents of this plan complained that a Council policy required the money to be spent on resolving the car parking shortage in the centre of the town. This was even more essential to combat the competition of the new giant Castlepoint development on Castle Lane where there are over 3,000 free car parking spaces. Beales, the large department store in the town centre, had reported to its AGM of shareholders that Castlepoint had dramatically affected sales at its Bournemouth branch.

The Council chose a firm in 2004 to make alterations to take the Pavilion building and its immediate surroundings into the 21st century and to run it in return for a 99 year lease. Part of the deal would include permission to build a Casino and an underground multi-storey car park. The town waits.

Further Changes

The Bournemouth International Centre will have £20 million spent on it for the enlargement of its conference facilities and additional exhibition space. Its large Windsor Hall will be extended so that the building continues to attract the world's top entertainment stars. The South West Regional Development Board have given the whole scheme £4.4 million.

Bournemouth has left its bath chair image in the museum; the Invalids' Walk of 80 years ago has vanished; conference delegates who criticised the lack of pubs to drink in are now spoiled for choice; the 10,000 university students and the thousands who attend the foreign language schools have helped to pull the town into a world undreamed of even a few decades ago. Local families have prospered by hosting foreign students; and nearly whole roads of houses within walking distance of the University have seen 'To Let' signs appear as landlords seek, quite legitimately, to cash in on the demand for student accommodation.

The 2001 census showed that Bournemouth has the fifth largest population of lesbians and gay people in England and Wales with nearly 80,000 people of the same sex living together. As many were ambiguous in their answers, it is thought the number could be higher. London, Manchester, Blackpool and Brighton and Hove revealed higher numbers. The demand, too, for flats, luxury and ordinary, is insatiable, and any house on a plot of above average size seems to be subject to conversion or demolition for replacement with purpose-built flats of a varying number of units. Many average-size houses have invisibly been turned into two or three flats; the only outward signs are two or three front doors.

At the beginning of the 21st century, the press printed pages about the hold-ups of traffic in Castle Lane and the time it was taking to ease the flow of traffic near the Hospital and at Castlepoint. This has been tackled with new road schemes, but at peak times there are still frustrated drivers.

But these are minor grumbles. Bournemouth is now a cosmopolitan go-ahead town. It has never been afraid to change, despite many calls for it to remain in the past. Its beaches, pines and open spaces are the visible evidence of a legacy that has seen it transformed from staid watering-place into a vibrant resort and working town that appeals to all ages.

Further Reading

An extensive list of books and booklets on the town has been included in this one: they all form part of the Story of Bournemouth.

Around Bournemouth (John Bainbridge. Frith, 2000)

Book of Bournemouth written for the 102nd Annual Meeting of the British Medical Association held at Bournemouth in July, 1934.

Book of Bournemouth, The (David & Rita Popham. Barracuda, 1985)

Bournemouth 1890-1990 (Harry W. Ashley & Hugh Ashley. Bournemouth Borough Council, 1990)

Bournemouth Coronation Festivities, 1902

Bournemouth in Old Photographs (Michael Coleman. Sutton, 1989)

Bournemouth in Old Picture Postcards (Catherine Rothwell. European Library, 1990)

Bournemouth International Festival Programme (7-14 June, 1991)

Bournemouth Mayors 1890–2000 (Keith Rawlings. Mayor's Charities, 1999)

Bournemouth Mayors, Lives and Times of the (ed. Ron Whittaker & Peter Challen. Bournemouth Council, 2000)

Bournemouth Past (Elizabeth Edwards. Phillimore, 1998)

Bournemouth Planning Information Handbook (Burrows)

Bournemouth Song Book, The (Cumberland Clark. Wilding, 1929)

Bournemouth St. Peter's (Ian McQueen. Dorset Publishing, 1971)

Bournemouth Tourism Department Guides & Publications -

Bournemouth Firemen at War (Ted Hughes. Dorset Publishing, 1991)

Bournemouth Yesterday and Today (Anthony Light and Gerald Ponting. Charlewood Press, 2003)

Bournemouth, A Pictorial & Descriptive Guide to the Unexplained (Ward, Lock) (Dick Sheppard. Public Relations Dept., Town Hall, Bournemouth, 1980)

Bournemouth, Then & Now (John Peters, David Couling, Michael Ridley. Blandford Press, 1978)

Bournemouth, Welcome to (Bournemouth Borough Council)

Bournemouth: The Good Old Days (Rodney Legg. Halsgrove, 2003)

Bournemouth:1810-1910 (C.H. Mate and C. Riddle. W Mate, 1910)

Bright's Illustrated Guide to Bournemouth (ed. Arthur Atkinson)

Bright's Illustrated Guide to Bournemouth (ed. Octavius Curtis, 1888)

Bright's Map of Bournemouth with Index (Bright, 1893)

Britain in Old Photographs: Bournemouth (Alison Crawford. Sutton, 1998)

Bygone Bournemouth (Mary Davenport. Phillimore, 1988)

Century of Bournemouth, A (Louise Perrin. Sutton, 2002)

Conservation Areas and Walks in the Town (Produced by the Planning Department and by the Leisure Services of Bournemouth Borough Council, 2000)

Dorset in Wartime: 50th Anniversary D-Day (Dorset Tourism, 1994)

Down Your Way: An A-Z of Daily Echo Country (ed. Ed Perkins & Peter Tate. Daily Echo, 2003)

Fancy Fair Album of Bournemouth Views, The (Engraved for J.E. Beale, 1888)

Fortune and a Family: Bournemouth and the Cooper Deans (George Bruce. Laverstock, 1987)

From Harbour to Harbour: Christchurch, Bournemouth and Poole (Mrs. Arthur Bell. G. Bell, 1916)

Furlough in Bournemouth (Bournemouth Tourism)

Hengistbury Head: Draft Management Plan (Bournemouth Council, June, 1996)

Historical Souvenir of the Visit of HRH The Prince of Wales to Bournemouth, 19th October, 1927 (County Borough of Bournemouth)

History of Bournemouth, A (Elizabeth Edwards. 1981)

Holdenhurst, Mother of Bournemouth (Kathleen M. Chilver, 1956)

Literary Associations of Bournemouth, Some (C.H. Mate)

Literary Dorset (Rodney Legg. Dorset Publishing, 1990)

Medical Aspects of Bournemouth and its Surroundings, The (Dr. Horace Dobell)

Memories of Bournemouth (Andrew Mitchell, Andrew Hawkes, Ann Ramsdale. True North Books, 1999)

Penny Guide to Bournemouth, The (Albert Sharwood. T.I. Powell)

Please May I Cross the Yard? The Story of Alma Road School, Bournemouth, 1908-1940 (Margaret Bard. Author, 1993)

Proposal by the Bournemouth & District Civic Society for Bournemouth Inner Town Conservation Areas (ed. Paul Munro-Walker)

Reflections of Strouden Park Bournemouth and its Surrounding District (Yvonne Khan. Finial Publishing, 2003)

Royal Bath Hotel (Peter Pugh. Cambridge Business, 1988)

So Fair A House: The Story of the Russell-Cotes Art Gallery and Museum, Bournemouth (Simon Olding & Shaun Garner. Bournemouth Borough Council, 1997)

Souvenir, Bournemouth, Royal Sanitary Institute, 33rd Conference. July 24th to 29th, 1922. (Borough of Bournemouth 1922)

St. Peter's Bournemouth (E.W. Leachman. Sydenham, 1915)

Stories of Bournemouth & its Hinterland (Leslie Smith. Author, 1977)

Story of Bournemouth, The (David S. Young. Hale, 1957)

Sydenham's Guide to Bournemouth (15th Ed., 1884)

Through a Georgian Window: A Record & History of Pelhams, Kinson (Joan M. Pitts & Wyn Watts. Purbeck Press)

West Howe Too! (Word and Action, Dorset. 1983)

Who's What in Bournemouth (John Garling & Joseph Sault. Bournemouth Times: Eric Putnam, 1938)

The following booklets about Bournemouth, issued between 1974 and 1999 by The Bournemouth Local Studies Publications, each gives great detail of the area or subject written about and they are excellent. All but a very few are out of print and not even the library has a full set.

Apprenticed to a Trade (C.A. & J.H. Miles)
Beale, J.E and the Growth of Bournemouth 1881-1905 Part I; Part II; Part III (J.F. Parsons)
Boscombe Yesterday (J.A. Young)
Boscombe: The Victorian Heritage (J.A. Young)
Bournemouth - Study of a Holiday Town (D. Sherry)
Bournemouth and the First World War (M.A. Edgington)
Bournemouth and the Second World War (M.A. Edgington)
Bournemouth Holiday Resort 1882-1908 (G. Barber)
Bournemouth in 1868 (William Mabey)
Bournemouth Memories (E. Read)
Bournemouth: Saga of a Famous Resort (A. Lindsay Clegg)
Bournemouth Theatres 1882 to 1908 (Graeme Barber)
Bournemouth Trains and Trolley Buses (W.P. Ransom)
Bournemouth Transport - The Trams (W.P. Ransom)
Bournemouth Transport - The Trolleybuses (W.P. Ransom)
Bournemouth Victorian Schools (J.F. Parsons & J.A. Young)
Bournemouth Winter Gardens 1882-1908 (G. Barber)
Christchurch Barracks (John Barker)
Cinema in Bournemouth, Reminiscences of (E. George)
Citizen Soldiers: Bournemouth Volunteers 1860-1908 (M.A. Edgington)
Education in Bournemouth 1903 to 1945 (J.A. Young)
Education in Bournemouth, Postwar, 1945-1974 (J.A. Young)
Ensbury Park Race Course and Airfield, Bournemouth (John Barker)
Farmer West and Muscliffe Farm (by his Son)
Ferries of East Dorset (A. Tully)
Flying, Banking & Music (Leslie E. Bickel)
Founders of Bournemouth: Christopher Crabbe Creeke (John Barker)
Fullerton, Lady Georgiana (John Barker)
Holdenhurst Parish Council 1894-1931 (J.A. Young)
Holdenhurst School (J.F. Parsons)
Iford Bridge (J.A. Young)
Iford on the Stour, Hampshire (Kathleen M. Chilver);
Iford United Reformed Church 1934-1984 (Nora and Jack Parsons)
Iford, The Forgotten Village (E.W. Barnes)
Iford: The Lost Village (F. Barnes)
In Search of Freedom (E.G. Bennett)
Kinson, Old (S.J Lands)
Kinson Parish 1894-1904 Part I and Part II (E. Bevans and M. Gillett)
Main Line to Bournemouth (J.A. Young)
Meyrick Park Halt (John Barker)
Music in Bournemouth, Professional (Eric A. George)
My Story (Pascoe Marshall)
North Bournemouth Companion Guide (J.F. Parsons)
Pokesdown 1894-1901 (J.A. Young)
Pokesdown and Iford Yesterday (J.A. Young)

Pokesdown and Neighbourhood 1895-1910 (E.G. Wills)

Pokesdown Urban District Council (J.A. Young)

Pokesdown, A History of Part I and Part II (J.A. Young)

Pokesdown, The Village of (J.A. Young)

Postal Services in Bournemouth, Outline of (J.A. Young)

Railway, The Ringwood, Christchurch and Bournemouth (J.A. Young)

Railways of Bournemouth and District (J.A. Young)

Scouting in Bournemouth, 1909-1969 (Don Randall)

Southbourne and Tuckton Yesterday (J.A. Young)

Southbourne on Sea (J.A. Young)

Southbourne, The Story of (J.A. Young)

Springbourne Library (D. Leeke)

Stourfield in the 19th Century, Reminiscences of (R. Dale)

Talbot Village, A Walk Through (I. Armitage)

Talbot Village, Wanderings in (M. Gillett)

They Came to Bournemouth (Rita Popham)

Tuckton to Wick Hams (1978)

Victorian Boscombe (J.A. Young)

Volunteers: The Bournemouth Fire Brigade, 1870-1929 (Ted Hughes)

Westbourne (Winifred M. Bray)

Wick (L. Popplewell)

Winton and Moordown (J.A. Young)

Winton and Moordown 1894-1901 (J.A. Young)

Winton Parish Council (J.A. Young)

Winton Story (Nellie Hoare)

Winton Urban District Council (J.A. Young)

Winton, The Growth of (S.J. Lands)

Acknowledgements

I am grateful to the following for permission to include illustrations in their possession or for which they hold the copyright:

Grahame Austin (Kitchenham Ltd), pages 31 (top), 87 (bottom), 96, 143, 147, and for the front cover illustration;

B.W. Barnes, pages 78 (bottom), and again on page 145;

Christopher Chaplin for the map on page 8;

Charles Elder (Bournemouth University), page 77;

Denys Garle, page 32 (right);

Mary How, pages 97, 146 (top) and on the back cover;

Bournemouth Library, pages 10, 11 (top), 13, 14, 16 (right), 18. 19 (bottom), 21, 22 (both), 23 (both), 24, 26 (both), 27 (bottom), 39, 41 (left), 42, 51 (left), 55, 59 (top), 61, 62, 65 (both), 68 (both), 70, 71 (both), 78 (top), 80 (top left), 82, 83, 84 (top), 86 (both), 87 (top), 91, 92 (top), 93 (top), 100 (all 3), 102, 106 (top), 107, 108, 116, 117, 118 (both), 119 (top left), 121 (top right and bottom), 126, 132;

The Russell-Cotes Art Gallery & Museum, Bournemouth, page 80 (top right, bottom left).

The remaining illustrations are taken from the author's collection and the Dovecote Press collection.

Index